D1223529

Praise for *UKEtopia!*

"Jim Beloff is largely responsible for the uke's popularity today. Jim delights in everything ukulele—its history, its design, its capabilities, and its personality. And he's written some wonderful songs on the uke. If a ukulele were to come to life, it would be a lot like Jim—a great big happy four-stringed guy with a lovely voice, a quick wit, and an infectious personality."

—**William H. Macy**, Hollywood, California

"I know Jim and Liz Beloff to be quiet, moderate, and humble people . . . but, reading *UKEtopia!* and learning about their 'daring-do' on behalf of a four-stringed, people-connector called the ukulele turned out to be a mind-boggling adventure! Their exciting chronicle begins modestly enough with Jim's initial purchase of a uke at the Rose Bowl Flea Market in California. But as the pages turn, you will be swept up by the two Beloffs in a whirlwind of purpose—rubbing elbows with movie stars and pop icons—bringing the little instrument to the attention of the world. Believe me, so captivating, 'uke' can't put it down."

—**Noel Paul Stookey,** of Peter, Paul & Mary

"Jim, thank you for sharing the fascinating journey you and Liz have been on, sharing the joy of 'the dancing flea.' Your connection to the Pasadena Rose Bowl Flea Market Martin ukulele you found years ago reminds me of my great grandfather's curiosity about this special instrument. His entrepreneurial spirit got us into the ukulele business in 1916. Your book will inspire more crazy uke players and collectors. That is significant, because the ukulele is often a player's first introduction to fretted instruments. And what a fun introduction it is."

—**C.F. Martin IV**, C.F. Martin & Co.

"*UKEtopia!* chronicles the whimsy and adventure of the Beloffs' journey making a creative life in music through the most approachable of instruments—the diminutive ukulele. Through their affinity for this humble and ineffably charming instrument, they've shared a message that a life with self-made music is a joy to all."

—**Andy Powers**, Taylor Guitars Chief Instrument Designer

"I thought *UKEtopia!* was going to be about how Liz and Jim Beloff discovered the uku-lele. Within a few pages, however, it became clear that it was more than that. *UKEtopia!* is the origin story of the ukulele's Third Wave. What I love about *UKEtopia!*—beyond the colorful characters, fun anecdotes, and zany palindromes—is that music always plays the leading role. This could have been a book about business, networking, licensing, and royalties. But instead, it's a book about *music*. It's the story of how Liz and Jim Beloff's love of song changed the world for the better."

—**James Hill**, Renowned ukulele performer and teacher

"What a blast! More than just a fascinating and fun autobiography of one of modern uku-lele's most important figures, Jim Beloff's *UKEtopia!* offers a definitive look at the evolu-tion of the instrument's current 'Third Wave,' now global in scope and still growing. No one has brought more attention and respectability to the ukulele. This book details Jim's amazing journey, and also feels like an affectionate love letter to the friendly four-string."

—**Blair Jackson**, Editor, *Ukulele* magazine

"Jim Beloff has been mainland America's foremost proponent of all things ukulele since the 1990s and continues to hold that position with his work as a published author, com-poser, recording artist, record producer, book publisher, and performing artist. With *UKEtopia!*, he tells (almost) all about the origins of his ukulele enterprises and shares some revealing 'behind the scenes' tales as well! Count *UKEtopia!* as an important addition to the ukulele bookshelf."

—**John Berger**, Editor, *Hawaiian Music and Musicians*, Second Edition

"I remember well the day Jim told me he'd be leaving *Billboard*. I was crushed, as we'd become best friends and inveterate laugh-sharers during our time there. But walking out one door and in through another has rarely yielded such a wonderful 'second life' career arc as Jim's—or such an engaging, warm-hearted story as the one told here. This book is Jim's generous way of paying forward all the blessings the humble little instrument has bestowed on him over the years. Reading it is informative, entertaining, and definitely a feel-good experience. How could it be anything else?"

—**Gene Sculatti**, Editor of *The Catalog of Cool*

"What an entertaining book! Jim Beloff's story is living proof that if you do what you love (and have a little bit of luck . . . and a simpatico spouse) you can't go wrong."

— **Leonard Maltin**, Film critic and historian

"Jim's stories are inspiring and full of joy. A great read!"

— **Tony Coleman**, Director of the film, *Mighty Uke*

"Thank you, Jim, for this most delightful book about the most delightful of instruments. If you love the ukulele, you will love this book."

— **Roz Chast**, Cartoonist

"If you love songwriting, if you love the ukulele, or if you just love a good love story—this book is for you!"

— **Cathy Fink & Marcy Marxer**, GRAMMY Award Winners, uke lovers

"No matter what kind of work you do, or what kind of business you are in, this is a fascinating read. See how a single impulsive flea market purchase changed the life and career of an enterprising man and his equally enthusiastic enterprising wife."

— **Christine Lavin**, Singer/songwriter and videographer

"A fascinating insight into the ukulele renaissance from the man who led it and a must-read for ukulele enthusiasts everywhere."

— **Cameron Murray**, Publisher/editor of *Kamuke* Magazine

"In telling the intriguing and unlikely story of how an off-off-Broadway composer/lyricist and advertising executive became a ukulele entrepreneur, Jim Beloff reveals the inside story of the ukulele's modern revival. In his breezy, entertaining style, Jim describes his and his wife Liz's pioneering labor of love as songbook publishers, instrument promoters, and performers that played a key role in fostering a four-stringed international phenomenon. *UKEtopia!* is packed with personal anecdotes about everyone from Tiny Tim, Lyle Ritz, and Herb Ohta to George Harrison, Eddie Vedder, and Bette Midler. An important historical document and a must-have for every ukulele enthusiast."

— **Jim Tranquada**, Author of *The 'Ukulele—A History*

"I had the best time going down the ukulele rabbit hole and discovering the 'rare-air' of Jim and Liz Beloff's passionate ardor for the ukulele and for the people who populate the close-knit, welcoming world of uke-musicality. If, as the saying goes, 'God Is in the Details,' then Jim Beloff should be canonized. The pure delight he takes in the intricacies of the lore, the legends, the history, the specifications of each style of ukulele is infectious."

—**Stuart Ross**, Writer/director of *Forever Plaid)*

"*UKEtopia!*'s story explains why young Jim Beloff was destined to be a major force in re-popularizing Hawai'i's 'jumping flea.' Who knew you could do all that with the ukulele? Jim did, although it took some time before he realized it. His attraction to the instrument, an eclectic appreciation of music, a keen entrepreneurial spirit, and the aid of his talented wife, Liz, helped to super-charge the current 'Third Wave' of ukulele popularity. This approach has opened wide the eyes of many people to the 'uke,' so now just about anything goes. Pop, show tunes, jazz, folk rock, classical, bluegrass, old time country, metal, grunge, you name it—Hawai'i's little 'ookulele' has a place. And Jumpin' Jim Beloff has been one of its finest ambassadors."

—**Stan Werbin**, Founder and owner of Elderly Instruments

"*UKEtopia!* is for anyone who has picked up a ukulele and found out they can't put it down. In these pages, Jim Beloff describes how the uke changed his life, and how he helped change the course of ukulele history."

—**Matt Warnes**, Editor of *UKE* magazine

"A great account of what it was like to be on the ground floor of the third wave of the ukulele revolution. You've heard of 'The Road Not Taken'—well, Jim Beloff did take it—and made a helluva difference."

—**Peter Brooke Turner**, Ukulele Orchestra of Great Britain

"Jim Beloff helped take the ukulele from a punchline to a global revolution. Twenty years ago, after meeting Jim, I became a committed uke player myself, inspired by his infectious passion. I'm reminded of a song I learned from a book Jim published and which best describes Beloff himself: 'Beautiful Dreamer.' God bless Jim Beloff."

—**Joe Hagan**, author of *Sticky Fingers: The Life and Times of Jann Wenner and Rolling Stone Magazine*

". . . This epic tome, documenting Jim Beloff's life in music and ukulele, has not only enthused many ukulele players, but his approach to the music business has doubtless inspired many entrepreneurs. I, myself, have learned much from the opportunities to work with Jim and Liz as a performer, arranger, and co-producer, and wish them continued success!"

— **Randy Wong,** WAITIKI International LLC

"Jim Beloff is the Guru of the Uke, an expert player, writer, historian, teacher, editor, arranger, and, along with his equally talented wife, Liz, the publisher of innumerable songbooks, videos, and instruction manuals. If there is anything about the ukulele or its myriad players that he doesn't know, then it's not worth knowing. This memoir covers his professional life, from his days at *Billboard*, through his growing ukulele obsession and the amazing musicians (Leonard Bernstein, Tiny Tim, George Harrison, Dick Dale, Merv Griffin, and so many more) that he has encountered in his nearly fifty-year career. It's a lively and fascinating book that will give you untold insights into this popular little 'jumping flea.'"

— **Happy Traum**, Homespun, Woodstock, New York

UKEtopia!

Adventures in the Ukulele World

Jim Beloff

Edited by
Ronny S. Schiff

Backbeat
Books

GUILFORD, CONNECTICUT

To Liz, my partner in all things.

An imprint of Globe Pequot, the trade division of
The Rowman & Littlefield Publishing Group, Inc.
4501 Forbes Blvd., Ste. 200
Lanham, MD 20706
www.rowman.com

Distributed by NATIONAL BOOK NETWORK

Cover Photo by Elizabeth Maihock Beloff

British Library Cataloguing in Publication Information available

Library of Congress Cataloging-in-Publication Data

Names: Beloff, Jim, 1955- author. | Schiff, Ronny S. editor.
Title: Uketopia! : adventures in the ukulele world / Jim Beloff ; edited by Ronny S. Schiff.
Description: Guilford, Connecticut : Backbeat, 2021. | Includes index.
Identifiers: LCCN 2021020805 (print) | LCCN 2021020806 (ebook) | ISBN 9781493060993 (cloth) |
   ISBN 9781493061006 (epub)
Subjects: LCSH: Ukulele—Anecdotes.
Classification: LCC ML1015.U5 B46 2021 (print) | LCC ML1015.U5 (ebook) |
   DDC 787.8/919—dc23
LC record available at https://lccn.loc.gov/2021020805
LC ebook record available at https://lccn.loc.gov/2021020806

About the Author

Jim Beloff is the author of *The Ukulele—A Visual History* (Backbeat Books) and author, arranger, and publisher of the *Jumpin' Jim's* series of ukulele songbooks with over one million copies in print. This series is available worldwide and includes *The Daily Ukulele* and *The Daily Ukulele: Leap Year Edition*, two of the biggest and best-selling ukulele songbooks ever published. All *Jumpin' Jim's* songbooks are distributed by Hal Leonard LLC.

Jim produced *Legends of Ukulele*, a CD compilation for Rhino Records, and has made three how-to-play DVDs for Homespun. He is also an active songwriter and has released several CDs. His two-CD set, *Dreams I Left in Pockets*, features thirty-three songs he wrote or cowrote with uke legends, Herb "Ohta-san" Ohta and Lyle Ritz. His album, *The Wind and Sun*, was released in August 2020.

In 1999, Jim composed and premiered *Uke Can't Be Serious*, a concerto for solo ukulele and symphony orchestra. Since then, the piece has been performed with both high school and professional orchestras, including the Michigan Philharmonic in 2016. He has also performed it many times with a string quartet. His second concerto for ukulele and orchestra, *The Dove Tale*, premiered in 2017 with the Wallingford (Connecticut) Symphony Orchestra.

Jim and his wife, Liz Maihock Beloff, own Flea Market Music, Inc., a company dedicated to the ukulele. They perform together playing their family's Fluke, Flea, and Firefly ukuleles. They have toured Japan, Australia, and Canada and believe in their company's motto, "Uke Can Change the World."

Visit Jim online at www.fleamarketmusic.com and facebook.com/jimbeloffmusic.

Contents

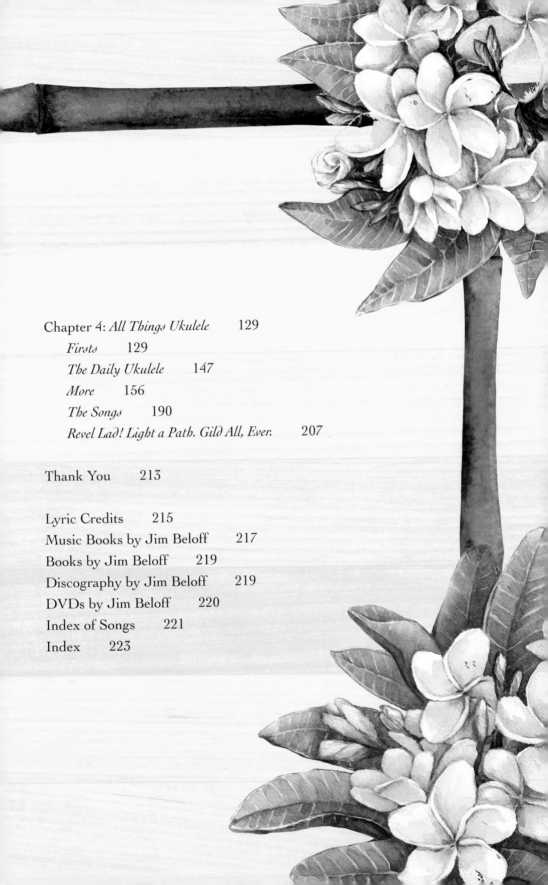

The author and Liz at the "Merv Griffin" house in 2001. (PHOTO BY FRANK DÖRING)

Introduction

Be Careful What You Buy at a Flea Market . . .

UKEtopia has been a kind of alternate reality for Liz and me over the last three decades. We stumbled on it accidentally one Sunday in January 1992 at the Rose Bowl Flea Market in Pasadena, California, when, on a whim, I decided to buy a 1950s-era Martin tenor ukulele lying on a vendor's blanket. During this part of the story, Liz usually steps in to say that since I didn't have the $250 in cash, she really bought the uke because she happened to have her checkbook with her. To this I would add, good point Liz, because let's face it, if she hadn't bought that tenor uke, this book might not exist and a whole bunch of other things wouldn't have happened either.

I like to tell folks to be careful about what you buy at a flea market. It can change your life.

It did ours . . .

1

Don Maihock with his wife Audrey in Middlefield, Connecticut, Summer 1991. (PHOTO BY ELIZABETH MAIHOCK BELOFF)

Chapter 1

The Road to UKEtopia

At the Rose Bowl Flea Market

In 1998, upon hearing that his son-in-law was going to quit his well-paying job with benefits and go start a ukulele business, any father-in-law might have reason for concern. In my case, Don Maihock couldn't really say much. He was responsible for it.

While waiting in San Francisco to ship out to the Pacific during World War II, Seabee Donald J. Maihock visited a local pawnshop and bought a used, plain brown Regal soprano ukulele. During his time in the navy, Don learned to play the uke and became proficient enough to entertain himself and fellow Seabees. After his tour ended, that uke returned with him and was often part of family sing-alongs that eventually included his young daughter, Liz. Fast forward to 1991: Don's daughter Liz is now my wife and we are all gathered together at my family's summer house in Middlefield, Connecticut. In our cottage, Liz shows Don an old ukulele that has sat undisturbed on an upper shelf for decades. He tunes it up and launches into several Tin Pan Alley–era songs that were part of his repertoire from his Seabee days. As an experienced guitarist, I was impressed by how much music was coming out of this little instrument. In particular, the chords seemed to have a greater richness than I had imagined the four short nylon strings could produce. I made a mental note that if I ever found a decent used uke for sale, perhaps a Martin or Gibson, I'd buy it just for fun.

In the fall of 1991, Liz and I moved temporarily to Beverly Hills, California. My employer, *Billboard* magazine, the music trade weekly, was hoping we'd like living there enough that I'd agree to head up the Los Angeles advertising sales office permanently. At the time, we were in the process of renovating a half-floor loft in an old fur-cutters building on 29th Street between Seventh and Eighth Avenues in Manhattan. For two creative people who adored New York City, it was a dream project. That's why it was

3

so painful when Howard Lander, the publisher of *Billboard*, asked me to consider moving to Los Angeles. We couldn't imagine living anywhere else but New York City. At the same time, Los Angeles offered a lot of potential for us. Besides being a step up for my career at *Billboard*, it looked promising for Liz as well. When I met her in 1979, Liz was a graphic artist designing promotional spots and opening sequences for Hollywood movies at the New York–based graphic design firm, R/Greenberg Associates. When this opportunity arose, she was freelancing for Greenberg and had a number of contacts in movie marketing in Hollywood. Career-wise, there were plenty of reasons for both of us to move to L.A.

During our three-month trial residency in Beverly Hills, we decided to make a permanent move to the West Coast. Fortunately, two dangling concerns, what to do with our New York loft and where to live in Los Angeles, were both solved by Tommy Page, a young recording artist who had scored a #1 *Billboard* hit when he was just twenty years old. As a financial investment following his hit song, Tommy bought a house in Studio City that he had turned into a pad for himself and his friends when he was in L.A. Tommy was a longtime friend of a *Billboard* colleague and happened to be with her when we had a going-away party at our loft. Tommy instantly fell in love with our place and soon after offered to swap homes with us. For three years we lived in his home in Studio City, while he lived in our loft on 29th Street.

One thing we especially enjoyed in our Chelsea, Manhattan neighborhood were the many flea markets on and off Sixth Avenue. These flea markets would spring up in the warmer months on the area parking lots that sat empty during the weekends. We loved the aisles of antiques and vintage collectibles and furnished our home with many a find. When we moved to the West Coast, we were delighted to discover that world-class flea markets happened virtually every Sunday in the greater L.A. area. The granddaddy of them all, the Rose Bowl Flea Market in Pasadena, happened on the second Sunday of every month. It was our very first time there in early 1992 that changed everything for us.

The Rose Bowl Flea Market was situated on the outside of the famed sports venue. Portions of it featured vendors selling new items like tube socks and "As Seen on TV" widgets. We ignored that part entirely. Our sole interest was wandering the aisles of old stuff. In the early 1990s, the World Wide Web was in its infancy and auction sites

Left: Rose Bowl Flea Market poster.
(PHOTO BY ELIZABETH MAIHOCK BELOFF)

Below: Rose Bowl entrance with author.
(PHOTO BY ELIZABETH MAIHOCK BELOFF)

Lee Silva. (PHOTO BY ELIZABETH MAIHOCK BELOFF)

like eBay were still years off in the future. If you hoped to find anything vintage, you had to frequent antique stores, garage sales, flea markets, or maybe your grandparents' attic. To walk the entirety of the "old stuff" section of the Rose Bowl could easily take three hours, including a stop for a churro and lemonade ice from the many food carts. On that first visit, we passed a vendor with a ukulele on a blanket. Upon closer inspection I learned that it was a tenor-sized, 1950s-era vintage Martin uke. Tenors are the third largest in the ukulele family after sopranos and concerts. The price was $250 and the vendor, Lee Silva, was not interested in negotiating. As a former gigging musician, he knew about instruments, especially prized ones like vintage Martins. I remembered my mental note from the year before and, in the heat of the moment, offered to buy it. Fortunately, Liz had thought to bring her checkbook.

The Rose Bowl Martin tenor uke.
(PHOTO BY JOHN GIAMMATTEO)

Prelude to Uke

To fully understand why I fell so hard for this Martin tenor ukulele requires a bit of background.

Both of my parents were psychology majors in college, so it was inevitable that they would experiment on me. After finding little pleasure in piano and violin lessons, my dad, Marvin Beloff, tried a novel approach to spark my interest in playing music. Instead of forcing an instrument on me, he decided to take guitar lessons himself at a local music store in my hometown of Meriden, Connecticut. Listening to him practice aroused my curiosity and eventually I inherited his guitar and teacher. After learning a few chords, I started to write songs. By middle school, I was in my first band—"Sherlock Holmes and the Investigators"—and I wrote the band's theme song. Eventually the bright pop music of the mid-'60s led to the late '60s introspective singer-songwriter era, and I was inspired by artists like James Taylor, Carole King, Joni Mitchell, Stevie Wonder, and Todd Rundgren.

Another major influence came along in 1970 with the release of the *Jesus Christ Superstar* double album by Andrew Lloyd Webber and Tim Rice. The idea of songs serving a larger dramatic arc appealed to me and I began to think about writing songs for the theater. However, when I approached the faculty at my public high school about presenting an original work there, they were not supportive. In 1971, about to start eleventh grade, I transferred to Choate, a prep school in Wallingford, one town away from Meriden. The timing of the transfer was ideal. It was the first year that Choate began accepting day-students from the surrounding area, which helped to reduce the costs of attending. Choate also became coed that year. Most importantly, Choate officially opened the visually stunning, sculptural, I. M. Pei-designed, Paul Mellon Arts Center. The arts center would become my second home at Choate. With my newfound interest in rock operas, I wrote, produced, and performed in three shows, *The Brain*, *Wheels*, and *Three Blind Mice* in various spaces at the arts center. All three shows were through-sung and featured original music and lyrics, except for my senior project, *Three Blind Mice*, which I cowrote with friend and fellow student Peter Wingerd.

Writing for the musical theater continued to be my focus at Hampshire College in Amherst, Massachusetts. Hampshire was a new, experimental school that was part of a "Five College" area that included Smith, Amherst, Mount Holyoke, and UMASS-Amherst. At Hampshire, I wrote two musical reviews, *One Life to Love* and *One Life to Leave* (with narration by fellow student and roommate Gary Shrager) and the book, music, and lyrics to *A Stew Indeed*, a musical comedy written entirely in rhyming couplets inspired by the mistaken identity comedies of Shakespeare. *Stew* involved astronauts, rock stars, and cannibals and was performed under a parachute in the Hampshire dining commons. The band was made up of a group of highly talented musicians and me.

Right: *One Life to Love* poster.
(PHOTO BY JOHN GIAMMATTEO)

Below: *A Stew Indeed* poster.
(PHOTO BY JOHN GIAMMATTEO)

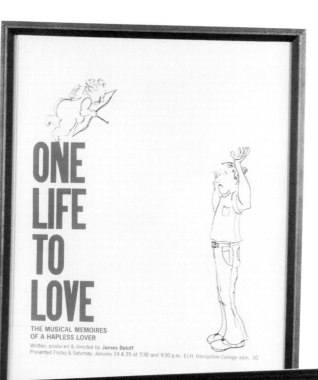

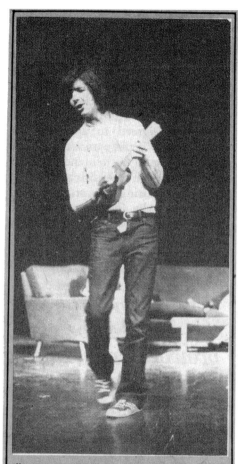

"Oh boo boop de doo," a musical comedy written and directed by student Ann Reddig was performed here last week. The words and music were composed by Sarah Weeks, a Division II student. James Beloff as Freddie, pictured above, plays the classical wimp infatuated with four women. Dede Burns, Joan Lanius, Pat Berman, and Robin McGalliard star in a lively Dick and Jane romp. 3/6/75

Oh, Boo Boop De Doo review from *The Springfield Daily News*. (COURTESY OF *THE REPUBLICAN*)

In addition to writing musicals, I was also notably cast in one written by two Hampshire friends. *Oh, Boo Boop De Doo* was about a classic wimp (me) infatuated with four different women. Two distinguishing characteristics of my wimpiness were an unzipped fly and, yes, playing the ukulele. I have no memory at all of playing the instrument, but apparently, I did. As my seventh-grade English teacher might have pointed out, this was a classic example of foreshadowing.

After finishing my second year at Hampshire in the summer of 1975, I approached the Wallingford (Connecticut) Bicentennial Committee about writing the book, music, and lyrics of a musical that would look back at the history of the town. We would cast adults and children from Wallingford and the show would be performed at my old artistic home, the Choate Arts Center. Thinking it would be an upbeat, family-friendly bit of musical boosterism, the committee responded enthusiastically, and I got right to work. The first thing I did was go to the Yale University Beinecke Library in New Haven, which had a treasure trove of rare books and documents including many related to Connecticut towns. While reviewing the long history of Wallingford, I discovered a remarkable story that cried out to be dramatized. It turned out that in the early 1850s, a branch of the Oneida Community (based in Oneida, New York) opened in Wallingford. The Oneida Community was one of several utopian communal groups that sprang up in the mid-nineteenth century, especially in Upstate New York. John Humphrey Noyes, the founder of the community, preached that Heaven on earth was possible because of the return of Jesus Christ in 70 CE. Today they are best known for the silverware business they started.

The Oneidans followed an extraordinary set of nontraditional rules that encompassed sex, marriage, selective breeding, women's rights, child-rearing, and collective criticism. They practiced a form of open or "complex marriage," where members were free to have sex with any other consenting members. The one thing that was against community rules was an "idolatrous" relationship wherein one member fell in love with another. My research at the Beinecke uncovered the true story of two members of the Wallingford branch falling in love with each other. Once their transgression had been revealed, they were separated and the one who was moved to Oneida eventually died of a broken heart.

When I went back to the Bicentennial Committee to tell them that I had found the perfect story to musicalize, there was an uproar. Even though the Oneida Community had closed way back in 1881, a number of the most senior members of the committee felt that the branch was still a stain on the history of Wallingford and that their bizarre sexual practices were decidedly not "family friendly." Fortunately, there were cooler heads on the committee who supported me. Because the musical, now titled *Two Sides of Heaven*, was so divisive, however, it generated an enormous amount of local press and daily letters to the editor both pro and con. I was either a young man following his artistic vision or an opportunist and pornographer who was looking to sell a lot of tickets. No doubt the controversy did help to sell tickets. The three performances of *Two Sides of Heaven* at the 770-seat arts center main theater sold out in advance. And the story became such a tempest that it eventually led to an article in the *New York Times* with the headline: "A Bicentennial Musical Splits Connecticut Town." The irony was that, despite the subject, the show was funny, touching, and respectful of the community members portrayed.

Right: *Two Sides of Heaven* poster. (PHOTO BY JOHN GIAMMATTEO)

Below: The author in front of the Choate School's Paul Mellon Arts Center in 1999. (PHOTO BY ELIZABETH MAIHOCK BELOFF)

One of the "you can't make this stuff up" moments from the experience was that descendants of the original members of the community who still lived in Oneida and worked for the Oneida Silverware company heard about the controversy and were eager to attend the show. Fortunately, they all had a great sense of humor about everything, were delighted with the controversy and nonstop publicity, and, most importantly, enjoyed the show.

Because it attracted self-motivated students, Hampshire was more like a graduate school for undergraduates. Instead of a major and a thesis, we had our area of concentration that culminated in a Division III project. My Division III was writing the score for *Down in the Dumps*, a musical based on the book *Suds in Your Eye* by Mary Lasswell. An Amherst College student, Sam Lockhart, wrote the libretto. Prior to that, for my Division II, my faculty advisors suggested I get some real-world experience working in a New York City theater. The idea, I suppose, was to get a gofer job or internship pushing a broom at an off-off-Broadway house. Instead, I wrote to three very high-profile theater people and heard back from them all.

The first, Joseph Papp of the Public Theater, was encouraging and invited me to interview there. Stephen Sondheim wrote to say that had I written him a bit earlier, I might have been able to intern on the pre-Broadway tour of his new musical *Pacific Overtures*. Then in late December 1975, while home for Christmas break, I received a phone call from Harry Kraut, Leonard Bernstein's manager. Bernstein wanted to interview me about interning on *1600 Pennsylvania Avenue*, a new musical he had written with *My Fair Lady* librettist and lyricist, Alan Jay Lerner. Three days later, I was in New York City in the back seat of a limo headed to LaGuardia Airport with Leonard Bernstein. He was flying to Washington, D.C., to conduct his *Chichester Psalms*. The interview went well enough for me to secure a production assistant position on the show and it even came with a small *per diem*.

From late January through to the May 4 Broadway opening, I worked in various capacities on *1600 Pennsylvania Avenue*. *1600* was a work near and dear to both of its creators' hearts. Four years in the making, it was a concept musical that charted the evolving relationship between the upstairs presidential families and the downstairs

Black families that served them. The show covered the years from George Washington to Teddy Roosevelt, and the score was ambitious and brilliant, and, by turns, catchy, touching, challenging, anthemic, brassy, and comedic. During the rehearsals in Manhattan, there were endless changes made to the songs and I took a lot of taxi rides back and forth between the music staff of the show and the orchestrators. I was also constantly updating cast scripts and, yes, running for coffee. On February 23 at the opening night in Philadelphia, I took notes for Bernstein at the back of the Forrest Theatre. As we watched the show together from the marble mezzanine stairs, he would whisper his dissatisfaction with the sound mix or a line interpretation or a vocal performance. Later on, I would hand my notes back to him as he reviewed them with the production staff and cast.

Due to conducting commitments, Bernstein was away for much of the Washington, D.C., run at the Kennedy Center. As a result, I made myself useful to Lerner who was holed up in a suite at the Watergate Hotel. Most of those days were spent in the hotel copier room with the constant script changes. By this point, the show had weathered a lot of negative press. The reviews coming out of Philadelphia were bad and the show had replaced its original director and choreographer. There were rumors that the show was going to close "out of town" and the cast was exhausted from the constant scene, song, and directorial changes and cuts. Often, when I would arrive at Lerner's suite in the morning, he looked like he had worked straight through the night. In the middle of one particularly bad night, he discovered that there was a fundamental continuity flaw in his libretto that he wasn't sure how to fix. I still have a copy of the memo he wrote to the show staff about that revelation. It's morbidly funny, but he essentially throws up his hands at the impasse. The show limped to Broadway, opened on May 4 at the Mark Hellinger Theatre to abysmal reviews, and closed seven performances later.

Ironically, my experience working on *1600* was invaluable, because it was such a legendary flop. It's one thing to watch Leonard Bernstein and Alan Jay Lerner create a masterpiece. It's something else to watch them work tirelessly and then fail. The teachable moments from that time still resonate forty-plus years later. And today, the seldom-heard score is hailed by many musical theater aficionados as one of the finest written by either man.

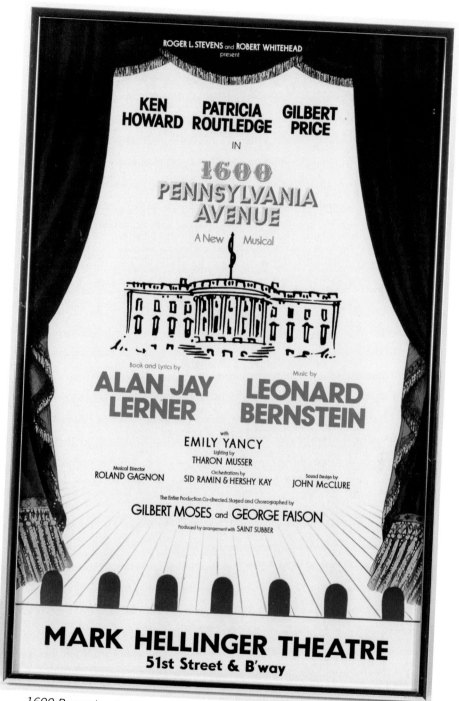

1600 Pennsylvania Avenue poster. (PHOTO BY JOHN GIAMMATTEO)

After graduating from Hampshire, I moved to New York City in hopes of forging a musical theater writing career. BMI, the performing rights organization, offered an invitation-only musical theater workshop for composers and lyricists, taught by famed Broadway conductor, composer, and author, Lehman Engel. The workshop had been the launching pad for several successful Broadway composers and lyricists including Alan Menken (*Beauty and the Beast*), Maury Yeston (*Nine*), Ed Kleban (*A Chorus Line*), and Lynn Ahrens (*Ragtime*). I applied as a lyricist/composer and was accepted as a lyricist. The first-year program was designed around writing various types of songs in a traditional musical. Assignments included a charm song, comedy song, musical scene, and ballad for characters in specific scenes drawn from well-known American plays. I was paired with a composer and we approached each assignment as if we were working on a real Broadway-bound show. We would present our finished songs in class and usually one or two of the presented songs would stand out from the rest. As I recall, our comedy song for Lola from the William Inge play, *Come Back, Little Sheba*, was a standout at that week's class. Ed Kleban was subbing for Lehman that week and we had him and the rest of the class in stitches.

Another memorable event happened after moving to New York City. Having established a slim connection to Stephen Sondheim while seeking an internship at Hampshire, I wrote him again in my senior year after being cast in a production of his musical *Company* at neighboring Mount Holyoke College. This was my first introduction to Sondheim's groundbreaking '70s concept musicals that featured his music and lyrics. In my letter, I wrote how much I was moved by his work and days later I received a note back inviting me to visit him when I had settled in New York. After relocating to the city, I called him, and we set up an appointment. He could not have been more generous with his time. I remember discussing *1600 Pennsylvania Avenue* with him, which, of course, he had thought a good deal about, given his close association with Leonard Bernstein. Then he asked to see an example of my lyric writing. Although he was critical of virtually all of it, I still recall the care in which he critiqued the work. As a teenager, Sondheim famously studied the craft of musical theater writing under the tutelage of Oscar Hammerstein II, and in my time at his townhouse, I felt that he was paying that extraordinary experience forward. To this day, his music and lyrics still move me like no other songwriter.

A serendipitous meeting on the 57th Street crosstown bus led me to a group of musical theater devotees who wanted to give new life to short-lived and forgotten musicals. Although I was only briefly part of that group, one of the longtime members mentioned my name to a producer/director of a children's musical series at the Hartley House Theatre on 46th Street. Lee Frank was the director of the *On Stage, Children* series at the Hartley House and she was looking for a composer/lyricist to write the score for a musical about a bag lady. Though the venue was very much off-off-Broadway, *Jennifer and Her Bag Lady* proved to be an ideal New York City musical debut for me. The story revolved around a teenage, city girl's relationship with a bag lady named Aggie Rivers who had been a vaudeville star. In addition to writing the music and lyrics for the show, I also played a blind street guitarist in the production, which allowed me to be the "orchestra," backing up the cast on their songs. Lee used her *On Stage, Children* series to highlight difficult subjects like homelessness and the show was a success with both kids and adults. For one memorable performance, Lee arranged to have a group of homeless women see the show. It was a profound experience to perform this story for the very people about whom it was written.

Jennifer and Her Bag Lady poster. (PHOTO BY JOHN GIAMMATTEO)

It's worth pointing out that virtually all of the shows I wrote at Choate and Hampshire, as well as *Two Sides of Heaven* and *Jennifer and Her Bag Lady*, were written on the guitar. The only exception was *Down in the Dumps*, which I consciously chose to write on piano. For most of the history of the American musical, the piano has been the principal writing tool for composers. All of my biggest heroes like Stephen Sondheim, Leonard Bernstein, Richard Rodgers, Stephen Schwartz, Jule Styne, and others, were all piano-based composers and I thought I should give the piano a try as well. Although the score to *Down in the Dumps* had its moments, I concluded that I was far more comfortable composing on the guitar.

At the same time that I was learning the craft of a composer/lyricist for the musical theater, I was also developing an interest in the great songwriters of the Tin Pan Alley era, many of whom also wrote for Broadway. I started collecting books about Ira Gershwin, Irving Berlin, Cole Porter, Lorenz Hart, Sammy Cahn, Johnny Mercer, and Hoagy Carmichael, as well as books of their lyrics. As a longtime fan of puzzles and word games, I was especially attracted to the rules that these lyricists worked within, constraints that involved song structure, scansion, and perfect rhyme. Another was ending a song with an open vowel sound like the word "you," which is easier for a singer to hold than a hard-consonant word such as "back," which requires the singer to produce a less pleasing "K" as the last sound of the song. A classic example of all of these considerations can be found in Irving Berlin's 1924 standard "What'll I Do." Here, Berlin crafts a classic AABA structure with perfect scansion and rhyme, expresses an original and yet timeless longing in under sixty words (not including the verse intro), sets a colloquial expression on a melody that reinforces the meaning, and ends the song with "do" and its open "oo" vowel sound. All of this from a Russian immigrant who learned English as a second language. The metaphor that the best lyricists were like fine jewelers carefully setting words (pearls) onto melodies (strings) was something I took to heart.

Between 1980 and 1991, I wrote several other musicals. Lee Frank brought me back for *Miranda's World*, a prescient family musical about a future United States run by a talk-show president. As in *Jennifer and Her Bag Lady*, Lee wrote the libretto, but for this show I wrote the lyrics only. Joshua Stone, a musician friend from my Hampshire days, composed the music.

I wrote four other musicals with three different librettists that were never produced. One of them, however, did generate a bit of interest. ASCAP (American Society of Composers and Publishers), the other major performing rights organization based in New York City, offered its own musical theater workshop led by Charles Strouse, the composer of many hit musicals including *Annie*. After being accepted as a composer/lyricist, I presented songs from *Abu Kaseem's Slippers*, a musical fable that took place in ancient Baghdad. Those songs attracted interest from Gretchen Cryer and Nancy Ford, the well-known composer/lyricist team who offered to mentor the project to the next level. The next level meant presenting a half-hour of the show at the Dramatists Guild in front of a panel of theater luminaries including Stephen Sondheim and Stephen Schwartz. Soon after gaining Cryer and Ford's interest, however, I made the regrettable decision to turn the show into a fully sung-through work, a challenge for even the most experienced composer/lyricists. I was way out of my depth and despite a few very positive comments, the thirty-minute presentation was a bust. This became a major turning point for me, and I began to rethink my long-term career goals.

To pay the bills while I was in New York, I held several jobs. The longest one was selling advertising for Ziff-Davis Publishing, a leader in special interest magazines like *Boating*, *Car and Driver*, *Stereo Review*, and, later on, a profusion of personal computer publications such as *PC Magazine* and *MacUser*. After distinguishing myself in the classified advertising department, I was enrolled in the company's legendary ad sales program. William Ziff, who owned and led the company, developed the program over many long evenings with his top lieutenants who approached the selling of ad space as a highly structured, opportunity-directed dialogue between the advertising representative and the advertiser. Much in the way I loved word games and puzzles and songwriting constraints, I embraced structured selling and soon Ziff-Davis was moving me up the management ladder on several of their personal computer magazines.

Nearing my tenth year at Ziff-Davis, the company was looking to promote me yet again, but this time to Boston for a top ad sales management position on *PC Week*, a very successful corporate computing magazine. What *PC Week* didn't know was that I had already been offered a job at *Billboard* magazine which would keep me in New York and be much more in sync with my personal interests. At the time, however, Ziff-Davis had a vestment program that meant that if I left before my tenth anniversary, I would sacrifice all the contributions the company had made to my profit-sharing account. This was no small matter. And so, to play the game, I rented an apartment in Boston for exactly the few remaining months before I was fully vested. *Billboard* understood my dilemma and told me I had a job waiting once I was vested. Of course, Ziff-Davis knew nothing about this, and I had many an awkward moment promising to follow up on my colleagues' recommendations of great places to settle down around Boston. Liz would visit me on the weekends, but that summer I was pretty miserable having to live with the constant deception. The day I was finally vested was a happy one and, knowing how much I loved music, no one at *PC Week* begrudged me for wanting to move on to a prestigious music trade magazine.

Once again living in our loft in New York, I threw myself into my new job at *Billboard* overseeing major and independent record label advertising. The perks that came with the job like free CDs and concert tickets, a seat at the Grammy Awards, and meeting some of my greatest pop music icons made up for a somewhat frustrating corporate culture at *Billboard* and a record industry that based many of its marketing decisions on ego. Purely from a business standpoint, however, my ten years at *Billboard* coincided with a very active and healthy time for the industry. These were the CD golden years, which saw huge revenues flowing into the labels courtesy of dedicated fans replacing their favorite vinyl records with shiny discs. It also overlapped with the 100th Anniversary of *Billboard* magazine, which generated its own historic and ad-filled special issue.

Just before *Billboard* moved Liz and me to Los Angeles, I had an opportunity to write one more musical. This time it was for TADA!—a well-respected youth theater in Manhattan that specialized in mounting original musicals performed by talented, multiracial casts of older kids for a family audience. The director of TADA!, Nina Trevens, was looking for a musical about a city girls' sleepover. I wrote both music and lyrics for *Sleepover* and, so far, it's been my biggest musical theater success, having been revived at TADA! more than any other show.

Sleepover promotional postcard. (COURTESY OF TADA! LAURA REMPEL GRAPHIC DESIGNER)

How I Met Our Editor

By the time Liz and I came home with the Martin uke, we were already settled into Tommy Page's classic California ranch house in Studio City. Partway up a hill off Ventura Boulevard, it had a picture window that overlooked the San Fernando Valley with an enormous window seat below that could accommodate both of us stretched out from either end, without touching. The house also had an office with its own entrance that Liz used as her graphic design studio. There, she often worked late into the night designing promotions for upcoming Hollywood movies.

My expanded responsibilities with *Billboard* were keeping me busy during the week, and on weekends, when I wasn't traveling for work, I read the latest issue from cover to cover or as I liked to say, "down to the staples." While I did, of course, bring my guitar out West, I hadn't had much time to play it or even think about songwriting.

The author and Liz with Barney at the Tommy Page house. (AUTHOR'S COLLECTION)

The last song I had written was atypical for me, an old-fashioned crooner kind of tune titled "Don't Get Unused to Me." I'd started it in New York and hadn't had any time or incentive to finish it in California. As it was, the song featured some nice jazz changes.

Today the most accepted tuning of a soprano or concert ukulele (the two smallest sizes) is GCEA. Unlike a guitar where the tuning goes from low to high, standard uke tuning starts high with the G string, followed by a lower C string and then steadily higher to E and A. This is known as "reentrant tuning" and when the strings are played individually from top to bottom it brings to mind the famous "my dog has fleas" melody. The biggest ukulele in the family is the baritone and that is typically tuned to DGBE low to high, exactly like the four highest pitched strings on a guitar. Tenor uke tuning can go both ways, with many professional players opting for reentrant GCEA. Some others, notably the great jazz uke player, Lyle Ritz, preferred reentrant DGBE, which was lower but preserved the "my dog has fleas" string relationship.

Almost thirty years later, I no longer remember why I started with the reentrant DGBE tuning on my Rose Bowl tenor. Perhaps it was tuned that way when I bought it. One of the first things that happened after I brought the uke home was I began to figure out the chords for my unfinished song, "Don't Get Unused to Me." As I felt my way with this four-stringed instrument, a song that seemed like an awkward fit on a guitar, seemed perfectly at home on the uke. The song practically finished itself.

The "Don't Get Unused to Me" experience led me to three early observations about the ukulele: The first was that the ukulele was the songwriting partner I never knew I needed. I began to compare it to Fred Astaire finding Ginger Rogers. There was something about the instrument that particularly suited the standards-inspired songs I wanted to write. Also, because the tuning was so similar to the guitar, it took very little time for me to find my way around it. Secondly, an instrument with two fewer strings than a guitar somehow, oddly enough, sounded richer to me. Regarding this, I realized that as competent a guitar player as I was, I rarely played all six strings all the time. At times, I would play five strings or four strings, depending on the chord and what sounded best. With the uke, I was strumming all four strings all the time. As a fan of close a cappella harmony and barbershop arranging, I began to think of the uke as a portable barbershop quartet with each string representing one of the four voices. I also began to experiment with chord soloing, where all four voices are constantly in motion revealing both the melody and underlying chords. Finally, I couldn't help but notice how much more portable the uke was versus the guitar. When I would travel for work to New York or Nashville, I would never think to drag a guitar along with my suitcase and laptop computer. A ukulele, however, was another matter—easy to carry and stow-able in the baggage compartment above my seat.

After a few days with the Martin, I decided to see what how-to-play materials and ukulele songbooks were available in local music stores. Sadly, I found very little. Music stores often keep their books in bins that are separated by a specific instrument divider like "Piano," "Guitar," or "Banjo." In Los Angeles in 1992, if a local music store even had a "Ukulele" divider, it either had nothing in it or possibly an ancient copy of a Mel Bay how-to-play book with Mel on the cover wearing a jacket and tie. In frustration, I decided to let my fingers do the walking and called around. Luckily, I reached the owner of a music store in East L.A. who thought he had some unsold uke songbooks in his back room, from the 1950s—the last time the ukulele was popular. Liz and I hurried down and met the owner who seemed to be in his late eighties and looked like he should have retired twenty years earlier. When he saw our enthusiasm for the stack of vintage

Some vintage ukulele books. (PHOTO BY JOHN GIAMMATTEO)

Three Ukulele Ike songbooks. (PHOTO BY JOHN GIAMMATTEO / COURTESY ALFRED MUSIC)

uke songbooks he brought out, he offered to sell us the store. We turned down the offer on the store but bought every old uke songbook he had. Some were generic "hit" collections with a stylized ukulele on the cover while others were personality folios featuring the smiling heads of "Ukulele Ike" or Roy Smeck.

One of the many lucky breaks we experienced in the early days was that Liz had been brought up on a steady diet of *The Lawrence Welk Show*. A weekly musical variety program that ran nationally from 1955 through 1971, *The Lawrence Welk Show* featured a talented cast of singers and musicians performing the best-loved songs of all time. Simply by being exposed to it week after week, Liz absorbed much of what is now referred to as the "Great American Songbook." When I was unfamiliar with a song in one of the vintage uke songbooks we brought home, Liz often knew it. In this way, I played through dozens of standards all arranged for ukulele and often featuring very ear-pleasing jazz chords.

Speaking of ear-pleasing, I should mention that I've always had an acute sensitivity to chords and chord changes. It must be part of my wiring. An unusual chord or unexpected chord change can literally stop me in my tracks, whether it be pop, jazz, or classical. As an admirer of guitarists like James Taylor and Kenny Rankin, I had long ago learned to play my share of sophisticated and unusual chords on the guitar. There is no particular reason why I should have been so moved by hearing similar kinds of chords on an instrument with two fewer strings, but that is exactly what happened. Perhaps it was the reentrant tuning that made the chords sound surprisingly closed and rich, but I found I was giving myself goose bumps every time I played through some of these classic tunes. I enjoyed it so much that I couldn't help wondering if there might be other players out there who would appreciate these arrangements if they were available again. But how? I knew absolutely nothing about how to publish a songbook.

Not long after finding the Martin tenor uke, I flew to New York for some sales appointments. One of the meetings I had was with Helene Blue who, at the time, was our contact for MPL Communications, Sir Paul McCartney's publishing company. After concluding my *Billboard* business with her, I mentioned my crazy idea of publishing a songbook of vintage ukulele arrangements and not knowing where to begin. Aware that I lived in Los Angeles, Helene had a very short and simple suggestion—"call Ronny Schiff."

By 1992, Ronny Schiff had edited at least a thousand songbooks for all the major print music publishing companies including Hal Leonard Corporation, Almo Publications, Mel Bay, and Warner Bros. Publications. She had personal contacts with all the major and independent music publishers, as well as a Rolodex full of graphic designers, illustrators, and music engravers who could help put a songbook together. After our introductory phone call, Ronny signed off with the line she still uses whenever we discuss a new project, "Let's make book." When we did finally meet Ronny, it felt like we'd already known each other a long time. One point of connection was that Liz and I were eager to learn more about our new hometown, and Ronny, being an almost-native Angeleno, was eager to share it with us. She began to take us on "magical mystery tours," where we would be introduced to her favorite points of interest along with amazing hole-in-the-wall restaurants that only an insider would know. In a very short time, Ronny felt like a member of the family.

Before we could start work on what would become *Jumpin' Jim's Ukulele Favorites*, we had several decisions to make. Although at the time, we were only thinking of publishing one songbook, Ronny recommended that we create our own company before entering into agreements with publishers and distributors. After meeting with an attorney, we decided that it made the most sense to set ourselves up as a California-based C corporation. Now we needed a company name. The one that Liz came up with, Flea Market Music, Inc., worked on several levels. We had found our "ur-uke" at a flea market, the most accepted translation of 'ukulele in Hawaiian was "jumping flea," and, of course, the widely known ukulele-tuning mnemonic was "my dog has fleas." Soon, Liz and I were co-owners of Flea Market Music, Inc.

The next decision was which print music distributor we should approach. Ronny had contacts with all the top companies, but she felt Hal Leonard Corporation would be best. Hal Leonard had an enormous back catalog of songbooks for virtually every mainstream musical instrument, but even more importantly, they had the exclusive print rights for many of the standards I wanted to include in our book. This meant that if I chose another distributor, I would not have been able to include most of the songs that Hal Leonard controlled exclusively. Although the ukulele was not particularly popular at the time, Hal Leonard was enthusiastic about our idea. The only other uke songbook they had in print was a decades-old Irving Berlin collection.

In our negotiations with Hal Leonard, an interesting question came up. Did we want Hal Leonard to publish the book and pay us a royalty for all copies sold or did we want to publish the book ourselves and have them just be our distributor?

Chapter 2

Let's Make Book

The First Songbooks

Because part of my job at *Billboard* magazine was to read it every week, I'd absorbed a few things that were helpful in our discussions with the Hal Leonard Corporation. One of the most common issues facing recording artists, has to do with ownership of their creations, especially when dealing with the major record labels. Often, because the label is advancing the costs of making an album, they end up controlling and owning the recording. As a result, these very personal artistic expressions are not the property of their creators. At the time, we were focused on publishing just the one songbook and we could have saved ourselves a lot of effort by producing the book for Hal Leonard in return for a royalty on the sales.

However, with artist ownership on my mind, I decided that the added complications of owning this songbook were worth the effort. Although I knew we would have to license the songs ourselves, pay for the printing and distribution of the books, and mail out royalty checks every six months, we decided to own *Jumpin' Jim's Ukulele Favorites* and have Hal Leonard be the distributor. Except for our *Daily Ukulele* songbook series, which is discussed in greater detail later, we have continued to own all of our songbooks and have never regretted the decision. And, after nearly thirty years, over thirty different songbooks, and over a million copies in print, we are more thankful than ever that Hal Leonard continues to be our distributor and partner.

This is probably as good a place as any to explain a bit about licensing songs and how that impacts the ownership of our various songbooks. When it was published, *Jumpin' Jim's Ukulele Favorites* contained a total of thirty songs. Most of them were well-known songs that are still very much in copyright. To include them in the book, we had to license them and all these years later we continue to pay "print" royalties for that right, and for the creators of those songs to be paid for their usages.

What this means is that while we own our songbooks, the ownership extends to everything other than the in-copyright songs that are featured inside. Most of our books include well-known songs by famous songwriters and those songs continue to be owned by their creators and their publishing companies. Just as importantly, this also includes any arrangements made of their songs. Those arrangements automatically become the property of the song's copyright owners. On the other hand, a number of our books feature only songs and music that have fallen into the public domain (written before 1924), such as early folk songs and spirituals and much of the best-known classical music repertoire. In those cases, our ownership extends to the entire songbook. For example, we've published four books of classical music arranged for the ukulele. All of the music in those four books is in the public domain and, as a result, Flea Market Music owns those books from cover to cover.

Once we decided to publish *Ukulele Favorites* ourselves, we needed to choose the featured "favorite" songs. Within the stack of vintage ukulele songbooks bought at the East L.A. music store, Liz and I found many contenders. Ultimately, thirteen of the final thirty songs came from three collections of songs arranged by "Ukulele Ike" (real name, Cliff Edwards) and originally published by Big 3 Music. These included arrangements of songs that were well-known standards, like "Over the Rainbow" and "Five Foot Two, Eyes of Blue," as well as songs like "Don't Blame Me" and "More Than You Know," that featured beautiful chord changes and sounded especially rich on a ukulele. Because I thought this might be our only songbook, I decided to include two of my own songs, the first song I wrote on a ukulele, "Don't Get Unused to Me" and another new one, "If They Can Put a Man on the Moon." Both were examples of my new Tin-Pan-Alley-inspired kind of songwriting. Another song in the book, *Whispering*, was written in 1920 and thus had fallen into the public domain. That meant we could include it royalty-free.

The size of the book was another question mark. We learned from Ronny, that the "Ukulele Ike" songbooks and many other vintage folios were known in the trade as "octavo-sized"—6 ¾ wide by 10 ½ inches long. The distinctive octavo format was especially popular during the previous two ukulele heydays, due to its smaller size and ease of fitting into a uke case. Although the larger 9 by 12-inch songbooks were the standard in 1992, we decided the retro octavo-size look would be most appropriate for *Favorites*. Fortunately, Hal Leonard was okay with this, even though bins in most music stores were designed primarily for 9 by 12-inch books.

One complication with *Favorites* involved the suggested tunings for these songs. Virtually all of the vintage books we found, including the "Ukulele Ike"-arranged ones, featured songs in a variety of tunings. A few were in GCEA, but the vast majority were arranged a whole step higher to ADF#B tuning, which was the dominant tuning in the 1950s. Because my goal was to have these delightful arrangements in print again, I decided to leave them in their original tunings. Today I wince a bit, seeing this hodge-podge of tunings, but I did make an effort to explain these inconsistencies in the "How to Use This Book" page. And, for good measure, we added a two-page GCEA chord chart. Also, because all thirty songs featured chord diagrams, I felt most players could simply ignore the confusing chord names and just play the fingerings.

Rereading my foreword to *Ukulele Favorites*, I'm reminded of my initial zeal for the instrument. It references how "smitten" I became after the "chance purchase" of the Martin tenor at the Rose Bowl flea market and how the "jewel-like arrangements" from "a wealth of out-of-print uke songbooks," deserved to "see the light of day once more." Also, "my belief in this project stemmed from the fact that every time I took my uke out at a family gathering, people of all ages would gather around to sing and/or learn these great songs."

Another big decision involved the title and cover design. This was the fun part. It's also worth stepping back a bit to set this up properly. Not long after Liz and I met in late 1979, we discovered that we both shared an instinct for marketing and promotion. Just for fun, we would invent product names and jingles for imaginary items, foods, and businesses. We also shared a great affection for commercial signage and advertising, especially from our own midcentury era. Because we both lived and worked in Manhattan, the city became an immense playground for our imaginations and we often spent our free time admiring the finer details to be found in the countless blocks of residential and commercial buildings. High rise setbacks with statuary, cast-iron facades, art-deco lobbies and elevators, Moorish tile work, and vintage neon signs became a cherished part of our visual vocabulary.

One early winter day while we were still in our dating phase, we noticed some people wearing earmuffs while other people were wearing Walkman headphones, a common sight in the early 1980s. At that moment, we both mused on the idea of a marriage between the Walkman headphones which had smallish orange sponge ends and traditional earmuffs which would then allow you to listen to music in the winter months while keeping your ears warm. Before long, we had imagined the product, the packaging, and the product name—"Hearmuffs!" This time, though, we thought the idea had real potential, and we presented it to a college friend of Liz's, Cindy Kerr, who also had a Harvard Business School degree. Once Cindy heard the concept she was on board and my dad recommended a small custom manufacturing company in Meriden (Connecticut) that could make them. Hearmuffs featured an eye-catching pewter lamé outer fabric and were designed to fit around the rim of the Walkman ear pieces. Liz designed the stickered logo that went on top of the clear plastic container and, with Cindy's business background, we determined a wholesale and retail price.

Hearmuffs in the box. (PHOTO BY JOHN GIAMMATTEO)

BEST BETS

*The best of all possible
things to buy, see, and do in
this best of all possible cities.*

By Nancy McKeon
and Corky Pollan

Listen to the Warm

Is your Sony feeling naked? Do you suffer from chilblains of the ear when the weather is blustery and you refuse to give up your Walkman? Jim Beloff, Cindy Kerr, and Liz Maihock—who didn't even own a Walkman—came up with the solution. Hearmuffs! The foam lining keeps your ears warm, and the pewter lamé makes the sound as good to look at as it is to listen to.

THE HEARMUFF COMPANY/ *R.D. 1, Box 441 B, Barto, Pennsylvania 19504/$7.95*

NEW YORK/JANUARY 11, 1982

Photograph: James Wojcik (Sony Walkman 2 courtesy of Sony Corporation of America)

Hearmuffs in the January 11, 1982 *New York Magazine* "Best Bets."
(PHOTO BY JAMES WOJCIK / COURTESY OF *NEW YORK* MAGAZINE)

The great thing about Hearmuffs was that they sold themselves. Manhattan gift shop owners would smile as soon as they saw the name and packaging, and, because it was just before the holidays, we sold a lot of them. We were even included in Corky Pollan's influential "Best Bets" page in the January 11, 1982, issue of *New York Magazine*. We might have had a longer run with Hearmuffs had we not received a cease and desist letter from an attorney representing an earmuff company that claimed that they had trademarked and used the name "Hear Muffs" before we had. Ultimately, we walked away from the product, but not before coming up with an alternate name: "Warm Reception." Ten years later, Liz and I were about to launch a new kind of product, a ukulele songbook.

It sounds a bit pretentious now, but all of my Choate, Hampshire, and post-college musical theater projects featured my birth name, "James," as my writer credit. This, even though my family and friends called me "Jimmy" in my youth and "Jim" in my post-college days. Because we had learned early on that "ukulele" translated to "jumping flea" in Hawaiian, Liz, after brainstorming a bit, suggested "Jumpin' Jim's" as a brand name. Although I was hardly known for jumping or any other strenuous physical activity, the name was fun to say, and it didn't seem out of place with other stage names like "Ukulele Ike" and "Tiny Tim."

Liz was enamored with the 1950s' cover designs of many of the ukulele songbooks that featured smiling "floating heads" of the arrangers like Ukulele Ike and Roy Smeck. With that as an inspiration and an assist from artist Elyse Wyman, who had designed hundreds of music books at A&M Records, she decided to pursue a retro floating head design of me for the cover of *Ukulele Favorites*. As a longtime graphic designer, Liz is also a type junkie and she had a lot of fun finding typefaces that harkened back to the '50s' songbooks. The boldface cover callouts like "30 Great Uke Songs," "And Many More," and "The Uke Is Back!" were also homages to the earlier collections.

Jumpin' Jim's Ukulele Favorites was released in November 1992, just eleven months after our fateful Rose Bowl purchase. For Liz and me, it was a completely unexpected first step into a new world. At the same time, it was also a profound learning experience, especially thanks to Ronny Schiff who introduced us to Hal Leonard and shepherded us through every stage of the book's development. Like the famous Chinese proverb, Ronny was teaching us how to fish.

Jumpin Jim's Ukulele Favorites cover. (COURTESY OF FLEA MARKET MUSIC, INC.)

In January 1993, according to an interview I gave to my hometown newspaper, the *Meriden Record-Journal*, I was already hoping to compile several songbooks and perhaps record an album of uke tunes. The article included quotes from Larry Morton, Hal Leonard's then national sales manager (now CEO), who claimed that the response to *Ukulele Favorites* was "surprising to everyone. We thought it might sell in states like Hawai'i, Arizona and Florida, but it's really been universal. From what we're hearing the key seems to be that it's been many, many years since anyone's done a ukulele songbook."

Thanks to the efforts of Hal Leonard's in-house marketing department, *Ukulele Favorites* generated a surprising amount of media exposure. The most notable was an interview on NPR's "Morning Edition" with Neal Conan on March 9, 1993. During the introduction, Neal referenced my discovery of the out-of-print vintage uke songbooks and said: "What he found enchanted him." Liz and I have had fun with that line ever since. There was also this exchange:

Conan: Do you think that we're in for a revival of the ukulele that I assume you hope to lead?

Beloff: I certainly wouldn't mind it. I absolutely wouldn't expect it, and I didn't do this because I thought that there was any possibility of it. This is more or less a labor of love, and if I can just break even, I suppose that I'm a genius, and anything more is almost too good to imagine.

I also performed a new song on the show, "Flea Market Monkey," my ode to our weekly addiction. Here's part of the lyric:

Ev'ry Sunday,
Finds me far away from home,
To the aisles,
That I love to roam,
Wand'ring through the bric-a-brac,
Got a flea market monkey on my back.

It was around this time that we learned that the "u" word, as Liz and I came to refer to it, did, in fact, have a bit of enchantment about it. After doing some research, I discovered that the ukulele had two earlier waves of popularity in the twentieth century. The first was in the late teens and early 1920s, courtesy of the 1915 Panama-Pacific Exposition in San Francisco, where millions of attendees visited the Hawai'i pavilion and observed native Hawaiians playing ukuleles. The second was in the 1950s, thanks to media superstar Arthur Godfrey and his various TV and radio shows where he often accompanied himself on the uke. The popularity of the instrument during those waves was significant enough that virtually everyone we discussed our new interest with was one degree of separation from a ukulele story. If they were older, they either had memories of owning and playing a ukulele themselves or they recalled a close relative who did. Most people our age had memories of a parent or older relative who played the uke. And, all of those memories seemed to evoke particularly happy, warm feelings.

Panama-Pacific International Exposition promotional postcard.
(FROM THE COLLECTION OF FLEA MARKET MUSIC)

PANAMA-PACIFIC INTERNATIONAL EXPOSITION, SAN FRANCISCO, 1915.

1903. THE HAWAIIAN PAVILION.

The Hawaiian Pavilion at the Panama-Pacific International Exposition.
(FROM THE COLLECTION OF FLEA MARKET MUSIC)

Arthur Godfrey promotional postcard. (FROM THE COLLECTION OF FLEA MARKET MUSIC)

On the other hand, we were also on the receiving end of a lot of Tiny Tim jokes and falsetto renditions of his biggest hit, "Tiptoe Thru' the Tulips." Eventually, I came to learn that Tiny Tim was terribly misunderstood as an artist and person. But at the time, his eccentricities and cartoonish performances on *The Tonight Show Starring Johnny Carson* were still fresh in the public's mind and inseparable from the instrument he liked to carry around in a brown paper bag.

Thanks, in part, to these collective memories, the story of an executive at *Billboard* magazine, the trade paper of record for the contemporary music industry, having a side gig as a ukulele book publisher proved to be catnip for the media at large. There's always a need for a fun, off-beat story like this, and I was happy to play along. Inevitably, I'd be asked why the songbook was selling better than anyone expected, and I used myself as an example. I pointed out that in the 1960s and 1970s, in particular, many of my peers had taken up the guitar, especially in response to the singer-songwriter era that produced icons like Bob Dylan, Paul Simon, James Taylor, and Joni Mitchell. By the 1990s, the guitar that they might have played in college had ended up in a closet due to the competing demands of a career and family. Despite this, many of these "lapsed guitarists," as I referred to them, still maintained some "finger memory," such as how to make chords and finger-pick. Once they learned that the chord fingerings on the ukulele were similar to the ones on the guitar, a spark was lit. Furthermore, parents with young children immediately saw the diminutive ukulele as the perfect gateway instrument to the guitar and the lifelong joys of making music.

It seems obvious now, but in 1993, the idea that the ukulele, so light, portable, and easy to play, could be just as satisfying musically as a guitar, was a revelation to me and to many new converts. Yes, the image of the ukulele still carried baggage, but with so many virtuosic guitarists around, being the only uke player in your town was a way of standing out at an open mic night or jam session. In addition, people smiled when they saw one, and when you played it, you held it over your heart. Also, in my case, Liz decided that the reason I liked the uke so much was that I could play it lying down.

Of course, the ukulele was most identified with the state of Hawai'i, and it was inevitable that we would visit there sooner than later. One thing we were warned about was the Hawaiian pronunciation of the word "ukulele." On the mainland, it was most commonly pronounced "you-koo-lay-lee." In Hawai'i, however, it was pronounced "oo-koo-le-le," and woe betide you if you slipped up. Locals were more than happy to correct you. Even the abbreviated version of "yuke" on the mainland was "ook" in Hawai'i. Like anyone who spends much time in the ukulele world, we learned to switch pronunciations at will, depending on whom we were with and where we were.

As it turned out, our first trip to Hawai'i occurred just after publishing *Favorites*. That's when we met Alan Yoshioka of Harry's Music Store, one of the most venerated music retailers in Hawai'i. Alan was Harry's nephew and his responsibilities included stocking the stores' sheet music and recordings. Ronny arranged this meeting, thanks to knowing Alan's cousin, Emmett Yoshioka, a well-known musician and conductor who was also Harry's son.

Alan met us at the airport and then spirited us off to a birthday party for Melveen Leed, an award-winning Hawaiian vocalist. Liz and I had just arrived, and, thanks to Alan, we were already meeting Hawaiian music royalty. For the rest of the trip, Alan would somehow magically appear at just the right moment to place beautiful leis around our necks and introduce us to someone important in the Hawaiian music scene. Alan also had a real gift for knowing which artists had the brightest futures and what they needed to do to get to the next level. On that trip, we met several successful Hawaiian musicians who gave Alan credit for his help with their careers.

The author, Liz, and Alan Yoshioka in Waikiki. (AUTHOR'S COLLECTION)

Alan encouraged us in the same way. He, of course, stocked *Favorites* in the store and was eager for us to publish more materials for the ukulele. Right before we flew home, Alan asked if I had ever heard of Lyle Ritz. When I said "no," he suggested I seek out Lyle's two jazz ukulele albums released in the late 1950s on Verve Records. Fortunately, Los Angeles was blessed with several stores that specialized in out-of-print vinyl, and soon after we got home, I tracked down both albums: *How About Uke* and *50th State Jazz*. Hearing the first track of *How About Uke*, a swingin' cover of "Don't Get Around Much Anymore," was like being hit by lightning.

Two Verve Lyle Ritz jazz ukulele albums. (PHOTO BY JOHN GIAMMATTEO)

How About Uke was recorded in 1957 at Capitol Studios in Hollywood, California, with Lyle on a custom Gibson cutaway tenor ukulele (tuned DGBE with a high D) along with three other top studio musicians, Don Shelton on flute, Gene Estes on drums, and Red Mitchell on bass. According to Lyle, it was the first stereo recording cut at Capitol Studios. Released in 1958, the all-instrumental album's subtitle was, "Lyle Ritz Plays Jazz Ukulele." The program was a mix of standards like "How About You" and "Moonlight in Vermont," plus two delightful, original Ritz tunes. The opener on side two was "Lulu's Back in Town," which would become Lyle's signature tune.

The *How About Uke* cover, from the duotone front to the hipster liner notes on the back, signaled that this was no novelty record. Here is a sample paragraph from the uncredited notes:

> And thusly the ukulele has passed with only commercial tolerance, beneath the upturned noses of critics and musicians, largely because no one had given the uke its rightful full share of devoted attention. Now, here in this album, is the delightful result of several years intimate acquaintance of a jazz musician with the ukulele—the results of which will surely excite critic and musician, and create new possibilities for the play-for-fun ukuleleist.

By the time I had finished listening to both of these recordings, I was transformed. I knew that if anyone who scoffed at the potential of the instrument heard what I had just heard, it would transform them, too. The word that came to mind was "cool," a word not normally associated with the ukulele.

Sadly, neither record sold well. Lyle was signed originally to a three-record deal, but after the disappointing sales of the first two, he and the label both agreed to pass on making a third. Lyle packed his ukulele away and focused on a much larger four-stringed instrument—the acoustic bass. Several years later, he had become one of the most in-demand bass players in Los Angeles as a member of the famous studio band, "The Wrecking Crew." Throughout the 1960s and '70s, Lyle played on thousands of albums by The Beach Boys, Sonny and Cher, Herb Alpert and the Tijuana Brass, The Righteous Brothers, The Monkees, and on and on and on.

In 1979, Lyle did unpack his ukulele for one particular gig: In Carl Reiner's movie, *The Jerk*, Steve Martin faux strums the ukulele while he and Bernadette Peters sing, "Tonight You Belong to Me." The actual uke part was recorded by Lyle in a Hollywood studio. In one of life's many strange coincidences, *The Jerk* was the first movie date for Liz and me. It was, of course, way before the ukulele entered our lives, but "Tonight You Belong to Me" would become a signature song for us as performers. Here was yet another example of "foreshadowing."

What Lyle didn't know and wouldn't learn for many years was that his two Verve albums made their way to Hawai'i and had begun to influence a whole new generation of players. For me, the albums were also a turning point. I now saw the ukulele through new eyes, eager to rehabilitate its image, and point it toward a bigger and brighter future.

Due to NPR's nationwide audience and some early newspaper coverage, we began to receive mail from uke fans and players from all over the country who were thrilled to see their favorite instrument back in the news and in a positive light. This was well before the internet, where a social group was just a click away, and many of those writing us thought they were the last strummer standing. By December 1993, we had sold enough of *Ukulele Favorites'* first printing of two thousand copies that a reprint was ordered. That month I also released my first album.

It's worth mentioning here that Liz and I were still working full time in our "real jobs" in 1993. Liz was working long days developing coming-attraction campaigns for Hollywood movies. As a film motion-graphics designer, she worked for several of the top companies in Los Angeles that specialized in creating "teasers" and "trailers"—industry-speak for the coming attractions you see at the movies. She would often work late into the night designing compelling ways to reveal the stars and title of an upcoming film, especially when there was little or no footage available. Sometimes, Liz created the title sequence for a movie, like the 1990 film *Home Alone*, starring Macaulay Culkin. She also designed several iconic movie studio motion-graphic logos including the one for TriStar Pictures in 1984 with Pegasus, the winged white horse.

Liz's storyboard drawing of Pegasus leaping the "T" of TriStar. (FROM THE COLLECTION OF ELIZABETH MAIHOCK BELOFF)

In the Line of Fire, a 1993 thriller starring Clint Eastwood as a secret service agent, unexpectedly brought Liz's two worlds together. One of the big revelatory moments in the film is when Eastwood's character learns from another agent that they remember a certain phone number because the seven numbers spell the seven letters, u-k-e-l-e-l-e. Eastwood even points out that ukulele starts with a u-k-u. Liz's teaser design for the film earned her a *Hollywood Reporter* Key Art Award.

As National Advertising Director for *Billboard* magazine, I was responsible for reaching weekly, monthly, and annual page and revenue goals and overseeing a nation-wide staff of ad reps. This also meant regular trips to New York City and Nashville for client meetings and executive planning sessions.

Despite all of these competing demands, I found time to release *Jim's Dog Has Fleas*, at the end of 1993. Clocking in at a speedy twenty-three minutes, the CD featured twelve original songs, two of which were instrumentals. The album was produced by Shepard Stern, a friend from New York City who had relocated to Los Angeles. At the time, Shep was an in-house producer for Walt Disney Records with several

Jim's Dog Has Fleas cover. (COURTESY OF FLEA MARKET MUSIC, INC.)

high-profile releases to his credit, including the *For Our Children — Benefit for the Pediatric Aids Foundation, Gumby — The Green Album* and Little Richard's *Shake It All About* CDs. Coincidentally, Shep was also a big uke fan and we included his "The Ukulele Song" in the *Favorites* songbook.

In a press release for the album, I wrote that "This album is just a natural extension of my continuing love affair with this instrument. While putting together the songs for the *Ukulele Favorites* book, I got inspired to write and arrange for the uke myself. Somehow, after all these years, I have finally found the right instrument for my kind of songwriting." The liner notes were written by my *Billboard* colleague and friend, Gene Sculatti, who had written two books of his own, *The Catalog of Cool* and its follow-up, *Too Cool*. His liner notes had attitude, as well. Describing "Sunday Driving," he wrote: "Verily it doth swing, and you don't have to try too hard to hear a Bennett or a Tormé hitching a smooth ride on it."

Other than a brief uke solo by Shep on "Dog Park," the album was just me on uke and vocals. I did overdub two ukes on the instrumental, "Ukelear Powered," which would go on to receive periodic exposure on NPR as interstitial music. "Lullaby," a song I'd written several years earlier on the guitar for Liz, enjoyed a new life rearranged for the ukulele. The title of the album, of course, was a riff on "my dog has fleas," and the cover, designed by Liz, featured me and Barney, our Welsh Corgi, who did indeed occasionally suffer from a flea or two. About the album, *Vintage Guitar* magazine wrote: "The songs are catchy melodies with crafty lyrics highlighted by that special ukulele sound that make you yearn for carefree days under a palm tree sipping umbrella drinks. 'Ukelear Powered,' is a propulsive hula jump that will get the grass skirts swaying."

In 1993, Hal Leonard offered "how-to-play" or "method" books for virtually every fretted instrument except the ukulele. In fact, as mentioned earlier, there weren't any uke methods to be found in most music stores other than reprints or new old stock from the 1950s, Arthur Godfrey era. Since *Ukulele Favorites* had sold better than anyone expected, Ronny suggested that our next release be a method book for beginning players. The result was *Jumpin' Jim's Ukulele Tips 'N' Tunes* released in May 1994.

Jumpin' Jim's Ukulele Tips 'N' Tunes cover. (COURTESY OF FLEA MARKET MUSIC, INC.)

Fortunately, by this time, I had accumulated an assortment of vintage method books from the two previous waves of uke popularity. Most of these books approached their task in similar ways, with an introduction to the basic concepts and then examples of songs where those concepts could be put into practice. With that structure in mind, we set about filling the introductory pages with all of the basic information necessary for a beginning player. At the same time, we gathered well-known songs where we could best apply those techniques.

We also added another key member to our team, Charylu Roberts. Charylu was already an in-demand print music engraver when Ronny recommended her to us on the *Ukulele Favorites* book. Music engraving is the art of graphically laying out songs and other music-related information accurately and attractively on the page. While Charylu helped us with several pages in *Favorites*, it was on *Tips 'N' Tunes* that she became an essential part of the team and since then has engraved every one of our music books.

Charylu then introduced us to an illustrator, Pete McDonnell, who helped out with the various technical drawings in the book. Pete's drawings were there to show how to finger chords and strum the strings. He also drew the "guy in the clock," which was our way of demonstrating the correct angle (or time) to aim the neck. The clock guy also helped address a common misconception about playing the ukulele. Virtually anyone who attempted to play the uke for the first time immediately started to strum over the sound-hole. I realized this was due to observing guitarists strum over the sound hole of their guitar. On the uke, however, the ideal place to strum is on the upper frets of the fretboard, not over the sound hole. We made sure the clock guy's strumming hand was on the upper frets.

Unlike *Favorites*, by the time we were working on *Tips 'N' Tunes*, I had made the decision that we would arrange the book entirely for GCEA or "C" tuning. I had confirmed that the preferred tuning in Hawai'i was GCEA and despite some adherents to the whole-step-higher ADF#B tuning, I decided that if ukes were tuned GCEA in Hawai'i, that was good enough for us. Today, it's hard to imagine that this was open for debate, but in those days when the uke was "off the pop culture radar," these were consequential issues.

Several things distinguished *Tips 'N' Tunes* from the method books of the past. One innovation was something I called "parenthetical" chords. I added these chords (literally in parentheses) to many of the arrangements to make them more interesting harmonically. Beginners could ignore them at first, and then add them in as they grew more confident. An example of this was the old folk song "Clementine," which would normally have just two chords in the key of C: C and G7. By adding Cmaj7 and C6, for example, it made the arrangement more interesting. Both of those chords also happened to be easy to play, with Cmaj7 requiring one finger and C6 requiring no fingers at all, just the four strummed "open" strings.

Another fun thing we did in *Tips 'N' Tunes* was to scatter little factoids about the ukulele throughout the book. There were brief mentions about well-known collectors, vintage recordings to seek out (like Lyle's *How About Uke*), and movies where the uke played a prominent role, like *Some Like It Hot* and *Blue Hawaii*. I even included a one-page history of the ukulele in the back. We also reprinted a 1993 ukulele-themed "Dennis the Menace" comic strip. I wrote to the comic strip's creator, Hank Ketcham, for permission and he was happy to let us include it at no charge. In his letter he wrote that he had been a longtime fan of the "half-pint guitar."

One other critical decision we made with *Tips 'N' Tunes* was that all of the songs were in the public domain, except for a couple of my own tunes written or arranged specifically for the book. This meant that we didn't have to license any of the songs or pay royalties on them. Over the years, *Jumpin' Jim's Ukulele Tips 'N' Tunes* has been one of our biggest sellers, and thanks to having no songs in copyright, one of the more profitable.

When it was released, Hal Leonard generated a press release for *Tips 'N' Tunes* that reveals a bit of the humorous, underdog position the ukulele still enjoyed at the time. They wrote: "Learn enough cool uke facts to mesmerize your friends and barrage your enemies!" And, "Add a second book to the ukulele shelf of your library!"

In April 1994, a month before *Tips 'N' Tunes* was released, I was promoted to Associate Publisher-National Sales at *Billboard*, reporting directly to the publisher, Howard Lander.

Something's Happening!

Also, in 1994, our ukulele world began to widen beyond vintage guitar songbooks. On July 31 of that year, I performed at the 24th Annual Ukulele Festival in Honolulu, Hawai'i for the first time. Staged at the Kapi'olani Park Bandstand in Waikiki and produced by Roy and Kathy Sakuma, the afternoon festival presented many of the finest Hawaiian players. The featured artists included Moe Keale, the Ka'au Crater Boys, and Israel Kamakawiwo'ole. Guest artists from outside of Hawai'i included Yuji Igarashi from Japan, the Langley Ukulele Ensemble from British Columbia, Canada, and me from California. All told, the fest attracted several thousand music lovers and families that showed up early with folding chairs and elaborate picnics to grab a shady spot in front of the bandshell.

Roy Sakuma was equally well known for his ukulele studios where he and his talented staff taught hundreds of young people how to play the instrument. While the featured artists received much of the press and publicity attention, the annual festival was primarily a recital for these young people. One of the highlights of every concert was hearing Roy Sakuma's "300-Piece Ukulele Band." Some of the children were so young that their ukulele actually looked big in their arms. They also were well trained and played their pieces with remarkable precision.

My invitation to perform at the fest was an acknowledgment of our efforts to promote the ukulele via our books. I do have a memory of performing a couple of my original songs and thinking that they didn't go over particularly well. Without a doubt, the star of the festival was Israel Kamakawiwo'ole, also known as "Bruddah Iz" or just "Iz," who had released his groundbreaking *Facing Future* CD the year before. By the time of the festival, *Facing Future* was on its way to becoming the best-selling album of all time by a Hawaiian artist, thanks in large part to the worldwide embrace of Iz's medley of "Over the Rainbow/What a Wonderful World." Iz experienced obesity throughout his life and a special lift was required to get him up onto the stage to perform. After the concert, he was moved to a table by the side of the bandstand where he signed posters, CDs, and ukuleles. Iz's personality and physicality were both larger than life, and it became obvious that day just how much he was beloved and revered by the local audience and, in particular the *keiki*, or children.

★ **24th Annual** ★

Ukulele Festival

Special Guest Star

JAMES INGRAM

★

ROY SAKUMA
300 PIECE
CHILDRENS UKULELE BAND

YUJI IGARASHI
(JAPAN)

JIM BELOFF
(CALIFORNIA)

LANGLEY UKULELE ENSEMBLE
(CANADA)

Also Featuring

KA'AU CRATER BOYS

ISRAEL KAMAKAWIWO'OLE

MOE KEALE

★

DANNY KALEIKINI
MASTER OF CEREMONIES

KAPIOLANI PARK BANDSTAND

SUNDAY, JULY 31 - 11:00-1:00 P.M.

Sponsored By

HAKUYOSHA HAWAII, INC
HONOLULU DISPOSAL
IOLANI/YOUNG HAWAII, INC.
YAMAGUCHI & YAMAGUCHI
FOODLAND
MCDONALDS HAWAII
DONNA WALDEN

YAMAOKA NURSERY
AT & T
MAHALO AIRLINES
SONNY D UKULELE
SEA-LAND SERVICE, INC.
KAMAKA HAWAII
ISLAND TERMITE

Special Thanks To

HAWAIIAN REGENT HOTEL   AIEA FLORIST   ADVANCE PHOTO DESIGN
BANQUET MASTERS   MOTOROLA COMMUNICATION
GREEN THUMB   TROPIC FISH & VEGETABLE

Presented by the Dept. of Parks and Recreation

FREE

FREE

The 1994 24th Annual Ukulele Festival poster. (AUTHOR'S COLLECTION)

The 1994 24th Annual Ukulele Festival. (PHOTO BY ELIZABETH MAIHOCK BELOFF)

Israel Kamakawiwo'ole at the 24th Annual Ukulele Festival. (PHOTO BY ELIZABETH MAIHOCK BELOFF)

The author, Roy Sakuma, and special guest star, James Ingram, at the 24th Annual Ukulele Festival. (PHOTO BY ELIZABETH MAIHOCK BELOFF)

Travis Harrelson (left), Chuck Fayne (center), and the author. (PHOTO BY ELIZABETH MAIHOCK BELOFF)

Later, in October, I performed at a music store in Huntington Beach along with the uke-duo, the DTs (Don Wilson and Travis Harrelson), and world-class uke collector and magician extraordinaire, Chuck Fayne. Of all the many unique and colorful characters we've met in the uke world, Travis and Chuck still stand out. We met Travis at a ukulele club meeting in a private home and Chuck at the Rose Bowl Flea Market while admiring a booth full of Hawaiian shirts.

After hearing about a group that met regularly in the Los Angeles area to strum ukes and sing old standards and Hawaiian songs, I was invited to attend a meeting. The group sat in a large circle in the living room and each member took turns leading a song of their choosing. I showed up with my Rose Bowl Martin tenor and a rare vintage National ukulele I had recently tracked down. In retrospect, the gathering reminded me of a meeting of the last true believers. Almost everyone seemed of retirement age and they talked about Hawaiian music with great knowledge and affection.

With a handlebar mustache, a devilish grin, and rapid-fire puns for every occasion, Travis was clearly the star of the group. He had a right-hand syncopated strum unlike any I'd ever seen or heard before or thereafter. It was so extraordinary in its rhythmic complexity that other players jokingly accused him of using some unseen sixth finger or third hand to create such an unduplicatable sound. Travis would patiently slow down his strum, so players could try to figure it out. But, no amount of describing, breaking it down, filming it from above and below, and even using a strobe light, ever really helped to unravel the mystery. Thankfully, in 1998, Travis agreed to appear as a guest on my first Homespun video, *The Joy of Uke*, and his unique strum is captured there for all to appreciate and analyze.

Travis was also a serious buyer and seller of rare, vintage ukes, and, after the meeting, he walked me to my car hoping to buy my National uke from me. Fortunately, I managed to resist his charms. And he wasn't the only rare uke collector in Southern California I met. I'd also been introduced to Andy Roth, who had a deeply curated collection of the rarest and most pristine vintage ukes. Andy was very knowledgeable about the history of the instrument and happy to share what he knew. And then I met Chuck Fayne.

It hadn't taken us long to learn that there were sizable flea markets to attend almost every Sunday in the L.A. area. The Pasadena City College Flea Market was the first

Sunday of every month, the Rose Bowl Flea Market was every second Sunday, the Long Beach Antique Market was every third Sunday, and the Santa Monica Airport Outdoor and Antique Collectible Market was every fourth Sunday. We started going to them all. One Rose Bowl Sunday, while admiring some vintage Hawaiian shirts, Liz noticed a man holding several ukuleles. She pointed him out to me and said we should probably get to know each other. This was the start of my long friendship with Chuck Fayne.

At the time, Chuck led two distinct lives. One was as a highly respected and very entertaining "close-up" magician, who appeared regularly at the Magic Castle in Hollywood, a private clubhouse for magicians and magic fans in a former chateau. His other life was as a buyer and seller of all kinds of antiques with a particular focus on art, vintage magic collectibles, and musical instruments, especially ukuleles. Chuck's personal collection ran to eight hundred vintage ukes, with some incredibly rare pieces mixed in. Many of these ukes lined the walls of the Los Angeles bungalow he shared with his wife and two young children.

While attending flea markets was an entertaining treasure hunt and Sunday outing for Liz and me, they were all business to Chuck. Over the years, he had developed a routine of arriving at a flea market in the wee hours of the night when all the vendors were waiting to go in and set up. He would find a willing vendor to ride in with and then start to work. Once, I got up in the middle of the night to experience this with Chuck and realized that it must be similar to a fisherman who gets up early to snag a prime location at a favorite fishing spot. Once inside the gate, and shining a flashlight, Chuck would call out, "any musical instruments?" Every once in a while, someone would yell back, "I think so," and Chuck would hurry over to be the first to see what might be nothing, or perhaps, the first crack at something quite special.

This was all well before vendors had a resource like eBay to check the value of things they might not know much about. Amazingly, there were times when a vendor would give a sizable discount on an old Martin because it was missing a string or tuning peg, not realizing that what they thought made the instrument unplayable could be easily remedied. Typically, by the time Liz and I showed up at 9 a.m. or so at the Rose Bowl, we'd inevitably run into Chuck who was nearing the end of his "shift." He'd tell me with a grin that there were no ukes left to find, he'd "hoovered" them all up and then would proceed to replay every dramatic detail of his morning.

Fortunately, despite Chuck's head start, and that of other early-morning collectors we met later on, there were still rarities to be found, and that is how I built my own collection. One day, we ran into Chuck who, as usual, said there was nothing left, we might as well go home. As it happened, the very vendor space we were standing in front of had two vintage Martin ukes staring up at us on a blanket. I laughed and said, "Well, I guess you missed these two!"

For my collection, I was particularly seeking out novelty ukes featuring fun graphic designs and cartoon characters, often made by Regal and Harmony and also oddly shaped, nontraditional exam-

A flea market ukulele for sale. (PHOTO BY ELIZABETH MAIHOCK BELOFF)

ples. Knowing this, Chuck sold and traded me many from his collection that were less important to him than the more valuable early Martin, Gibson, and Hawaiian ukes. More than anything, Chuck instilled in me the thrill of the chase and we spent more time on the phone regaling each other about our latest acquisitions than Liz would have liked. This led to her decision that she and I needed to implement "uke-free zones," set times when the "u" word was not to be mentioned.

Ronny introduced us to another fascinating and one-of-a-kind character who came into our lives in the early days — Ian Whitcomb. Ian was a rock and roll celebrity, a Brit who had scored a Top Ten hit on the *Billboard* Hot 100 chart in 1965 with his novelty song, "You Turn Me On." By the time we met him in 1992, Ian was well established in Los Angeles as a peerless interpreter of period music genres like ragtime, vaudeville, and British music hall and often performed with his band, the Bungalow Boys, while strumming a ukulele. In addition, he was a prolific author with many books on the history of early popular music and rock and roll, a passion and knowledge which he also shared on his weekly KPCC NPR radio show out of Pasadena City College.

Ian Whitcomb, July 2000. (PHOTO BY ELIZABETH MAIHOCK BELOFF)

When it came to discovering the joys of the ukulele, Ian was well ahead of me. He traced his uke roots back to 1963 when he bought a Martin soprano for $25 in a Los Angeles pawn shop, while on a summer break from his university, Trinity College in Dublin, Ireland. Ian was left-handed, but rather than restring the uke, he simply flipped it around and learned to play the chords upside down. As was the case with Travis Harrelson and Chuck Fayne, our ukulele journey would intertwine with Ian in all sorts of unexpected ways. There was no playbook to follow, we were simply making it up as we went along.

The Ukulele—A Visual History

By the end of 1994, my collection of vintage ukuleles was nearing fifty. Most of them were acquired at flea markets, antique stores, or by trading with other collectors. Also, at the same time, I was accumulating more methods and songbooks; sheet music with "ukulele" in the title or pictured on the cover; advertising that featured a uke, tropical-themed menus from the Matson Line ships that cruised between California and Hawai'i; and uke-related record albums, movie posters, and the occasional article or book that included any scrap of information about the history of the instrument. Every time I added something to the pile, I would think there must be a coffee-table book out there somewhere with pictures that I could cross-check with my collection. After all, there were multiple books about virtually every subject, and it was just a matter of time before I would find an illustrated history of the ukulele. It was inconceivable to me that there weren't at least several.

The fact was, sadly, that there weren't any. The only book even close to what I was imagining was a small, self-published sixty-four-page book titled *The 'Ukulele: A Portuguese Gift to Hawaii.* The book had three authors, one of whom, Leslie Nunes, was the great-grandson of Manuel Nunes, who had sailed to Hawai'i from the Portuguese island of Madeira and helped develop the modern-day ukulele. The actual text totaled four pages and the rest of the book was made up of sepia-colored historic photographs and a short how-to-play lesson.

The purpose of the book was to honor the one-hundredth anniversary of the arrival of the Ravenscrag, a British ship with 423 men, women, and children from Madeira, who arrived in Honolulu Harbor in 1879 looking for work in the Hawaiian sugarcane fields. The other aim of the book could be found in the subtitle. It was a pointed reminder that the present-day ukulele had Portuguese roots.

With the realization that there had never been a comprehensive book about the ukulele, I began to look at my own random collection of vintage ukes and ephemera, as well as other collections, in a more serious light. Suddenly the charms of a rare "Harold Teen" cartoon uke from the late 1920s or a Stromberg-Voisinet "Aero" ukulele shaped like an airplane from the same era, seemed in danger of being lost to posterity if they weren't chronicled in a full-on history of the instrument. The question was, who could write such a book? Although I had a decent collection, it certainly wasn't comprehensive, and after all, I was from Connecticut, as far away from the Hawaiian Islands as someone could be and still be in the United States. And, I wasn't trained as a historian, and outside of a few bits of text in our songbooks, I was unproven as an author.

The Ukulele—A Visual History might never have happened if it wasn't for Chuck Fayne's decision to move himself, his family, and his uke collection to Australia. It was stunning news for his friends, but Chuck had several compelling reasons why such a dramatic move was necessary. I knew at that moment that if I were ever to compile a book on the history of the uke, it would have to include photographs of much of Chuck's collection. At the time, there were a couple of photo-laden guitar books that I found particularly inspiring. One was Bob Brozman's *The History and Artistry of*

National Resonator Instruments and the other was George Gruhn and Walter Carter's *Acoustic Guitars and Other Fretted Instruments*. Because of the wide editorial angle of both of the books, some ukuleles were included in each one, but only a few. My dream book featured dozens of photographs of colorful and historic ukes and if I didn't move fast, Chuck's world-class collection would be on the other side of the world.

In January 1995, while Chuck was in the early planning stages of his move, I wrote a proposal for *The Ukulele Book: An Appreciation in Photos and Song*. The book would be a history of the instrument and also feature photographs of one hundred or more rare ukuleles and stories about the greatest uke makers and manufacturers. In addition, it would include the sheet music for a dozen or so songs that had "ukulele" in the title, like the well-known "Ukulele Lady," and more obscure "Give Me a Ukulele (and a Ukulele Baby) and Leave the Rest to Me." In retrospect, it looked like I was trying to leverage our recent publishing experience to create a hybrid photo history/songbook. A few months later, Ronny presented a broader version of the concept to Miller Freeman, Inc., a San Francisco–based publisher of music-related magazines and books. From there, the proposal evolved into a full-color, illustrated history of the instrument with biographies of the great players past and present, the uke in popular culture, and evidence of a new wave of popularity. By August, we were in negotiations with Miller Freeman for the first complete history of the ukulele.

While contract negotiations were moving ahead with Miller Freeman, we were thinking about other songbooks we could publish. At the very least, we thought we should put out one more so that we would equal the three songbooks Ukulele Ike arranged with red, blue, and green covers. That led to the next songbook, *Jumpin' Jim's Ukulele Gems*, released in November 1995.

With *Gems*, a formula had begun to emerge. The idea of compiling a group of songs that shared something in common. In the case of *Gems*, the core concept was standards with unusually clever chord changes. From the beginning, I was particularly drawn to the arrangements I found in the vintage uke songbooks that had a lot of chord movement. In the foreword, I wrote: "In assembling this latest collection. I pulled together well-known songs with, in most cases, interesting ukulele arrangements. Songs like 'Moonlight Becomes You,' 'Lullaby of Birdland,' and the five DeSylva, Brown and Henderson compositions feature much chordal movement and almost a jazz quality to the

Jumpin' Jim's Ukulele Gems cover. (COURTESY OF FLEA MARKET MUSIC, INC.)

arrangements. Every time I play through them, I am struck by the beauty of their melodies, the sparkle of the lyrics, and the brilliance of the chords. I'm also reminded of how great a very portable and outwardly simple 4-string instrument can make them sound."

In *Gems*, I even doubled down on my love affair with chord changes by adding six "chord solos" at the end of the book. Chord solos were clever arrangements where both the melody and chords can be heard simultaneously, and several of the vintage songbooks I had accumulated included these unique solos. Often, this meant playing a different chord for each note of the melody. Obviously, these arrangements were more challenging, but not beyond the abilities of an experienced player. As I wrote in *Gems*, "once mastered, these types of arrangements can be some of the most satisfying pieces you can play for yourself and others. They really become show pieces."

My creative involvement with the arrangements began to shift a bit with *Gems*. The cover of *Favorites* credited me as "editor" and *Gems* as "compiler." In both cases, however, my musical contributions were choosing which existing arrangements I wanted to include. I saw my role as an archivist, determined to make these beautiful arrangements available again. There were some exceptions. Certainly, the two original songs in *Favorites* and my song "Scratchy Records" in *Gems* were my arrangements. I also arranged two of the chord solos in *Gems*: "Till There Was You" and "When You Wish Upon a Star."

Something else happened in November 1995 that I interpreted as a significant omen. Around Thanksgiving, there was a three-night airing on ABC of *The Beatles Anthology* documentary in which the ukulele received an unusual amount of attention. Paul McCartney mentioned that John Lennon's mom played the uke and said, "To this day, if I ever meet grown-ups who play the ukulele, I love 'em." Later on, in the documentary, George Harrison is seen playing "I Will," as well as another tune on a uke. Here were members of a band that made every kid in the world want to play the guitar, showing some serious affection for the "jumping flea."

On February 22, 1996, I signed Miller Freeman's contract for *The Ukulele—A Visual History*. By then, I was well into the research and writing of the book and we had added several essential members to the team. Ronny would be the editor and oversee image clearances. Due to my *Billboard* and ukulele worlds crossing paths, I discovered that Tommy Steele, the Vice President of Creative Services at Capitol Records, was also a fan of all things Hawaiian and had written, photographed, and designed the definitive book, *The Hawaiian Shirt: Its Art and History*. When he heard about the uke book project, Tommy expressed interest in working on it and eventually agreed to be the art director and designer along with Andy Engel, an independent graphic designer who regularly collaborated with Tommy on Capitol Records projects.

Also, of great assistance to the book was DeSoto Brown, a historian at the Bishop Museum in Honolulu and owner and archivist of his own enormous personal collection of Hawaiian memorabilia. I first spoke to DeSoto at the Bishop Museum in late 1993, when we were looking for historic photos to add to the *Tips 'N' Tunes* method book. Our image requests were much broader for the uke history book and in the end, DeSoto helped us with more early photos from the Bishop collection plus sheet music covers and a photo of John Lennon and George Harrison in Waikiki from his personal collection.

In July, I was invited back to perform at Roy Sakuma's Ukulele Festival. That year the featured artists included Lyle Ritz, Herb "Ohta-San" Ohta, the Ka'au Crater Boys, and Moe Keale. Three years after hearing *How About Uke*, I was about to meet Lyle Ritz in person. Because I was still researching for the history book, the timing was perfect for me to interview several people including Lyle, who had moved to Hawai'i with his wife, Geri, and daughter, Emily, in 1988. He was an active musician on the island playing bass and, of course, ukulele. He credited Roy Sakuma for tracking him down in California and letting him know just how much he was admired in Hawai'i for his two jazz uke albums.

That week, I met Lyle for breakfast at the Sheraton Waikiki. We both brought our tenor ukes and it was quite a memorable time for me. The photo that Liz took shows just how much I was in awe of Lyle, who deflected all of my adulation in his aw-shucks, humble, and dry-humored way. Lyle played us a few tunes right at the beach-side table. In return, I played his arrangement of "Don't Get Around Much Anymore," which I had learned from repeated spins of the record. A fun factoid about Lyle was that in 1970, when he was at the peak of his Wrecking Crew career in Los Angeles, he acquired the 1940 Buick Phaeton convertible used in the final airport scene of the movie, *Casablanca*. He was a vintage car buff and took enormous pleasure in fixing and driving that car. So, if you'll indulge me, the breakfast at the Sheraton Waikiki was the "beginning of a beautiful friendship."

Lyle Ritz and the author at the Sheraton Waikiki in 1996. (PHOTO BY ELIZABETH MAIHOCK BELOFF)

My schedule for that week in Hawai'i included meetings with DeSoto Brown, Leslie Nunes (the coauthor of the only existing book about the ukulele), and Fred and Sam Kamaka of Kamaka Ukulele who also arranged a tour of the factory for us. Kamaka was the oldest and most respected of all the Hawaiian ukulele makers. We also met with Elma T. Cabral, who was the granddaughter of Augusto Dias, one of the three Madeiran men credited with developing the first ukuleles after their arrival in Honolulu in 1879. In a 1946 article in the *Paradise of the Pacific* magazine, Elma described in detail watching her grandfather make a ukulele from start to finish, beginning with the molding of strips of koa wood and ending with the insertion of the label in the sound hole. By the time we met her, Elma's memories weren't quite as sharp, but she couldn't have been kinder to us or more enthusiastic about the history book. Leslie Nunes, too, was very generous with his time, information, and encouragement. Between Elma and Leslie, I felt I was representing at least two of the three families of the original Madeiran ukulele craftsmen. As always, Liz was there to document with photos.

When we finally met DeSoto Brown in person, he shared with us how his collecting bug began. As a child, DeSoto remembered his parents dutifully throwing out the old phone book when the latest one

Elma Cabral in Honolulu, Hawai'i, 1996.
(PHOTO BY ELIZABETH MAIHOCK BELOFF)

Leslie Nunes and the author in Hawai'i, 1996. (PHOTO BY ELIZABETH MAIHOCK BELOFF)

Liz, the author, and DeSoto Brown in Honolulu, Hawai'i, 1996. (AUTHOR'S COLLECTION)

Herb Ohta in Honolulu, Hawai'i. (PHOTO BY ELIZABETH MAIHOCK BELOFF)

arrived. In his young mind, he couldn't reconcile throwing out the older book just because it was old. To him, it contained historic information that wasn't in the newer phone book. Then, as a teenager, he started visiting the lobbies of all the major hotels to take a sample of every offering included in the tourist activities racks. To DeSoto, each promotional piece was a snapshot of a time and place and worthy of being archived. Thinking back now, I'm sure some of DeSoto's thoughts on collecting rubbed off on us when it came to documenting and saving the ephemera from our own uke adventures.

Liz and I also introduced ourselves to Herb "Ohta-San" Ohta, who was a mentor to Roy Sakuma, and one of the most admired of all the Hawaiian ukulele virtuosos, especially in Japan. By the time we met him, Herb had already recorded dozens of lush instrumental albums for multiple record labels including A&M, where in 1973 he had his biggest hit, "Song for Anna." Fueled by the success of the title song, the album became an international hit, selling more than six million copies. "Song for Anna" was composed by André Popp who was best known to American audiences for "Love Is Blue."

Of all the top players we met in Hawai'i, Herb was the most intimidating. At first, he seemed quite serious and standoffish. I smile about that now because eventually we became good friends and I discovered that Herb loved to laugh and had a weakness for telling corny jokes. We also would become longtime songwriting partners, with Herb composing the music and me supplying the words.

Liz and I participated in one more memorable event that year, organized by the "Ukulele Hall of Fame." The nonprofit organization was founded in 1996, dedicated to the preservation and promotion of ukulele history and culture, and on September 28 presented Ukulele Expo 1996 at the Montague Bookmill in Massachusetts. The all-day event featured hundreds of rare vintage ukes on the walls of the basement exhibition space plus several vendors with various old and new offerings.

Attendees came from all over the country including Leslie Nunes from Hawai'i, who opened the evening concert at the nearby Montague Grange Hall with a brief history of the ukulele. Just over one hundred people turned out for the concert to hear Humuhumunukunukuapua'a, a band made up of the Hall of Fame organizers, Fred Fallin from Chicago who specialized in Tin Pan Alley tunes, me playing original songs, The Pinetones from Maine led by uke whiz and luthier, Joel Eckhaus, and, finally, the headliner, Tiny Tim. After his introduction, Tiny Tim emerged looking a bit disoriented, and said: "If you happen to hear any coughing during the performance . . . well that's because . . . well, you know . . . ," and then fell off the stage face-down while still holding his metal-body resonator uke. It says something about Tiny Tim's unusual career that for a few stunned seconds, there were those in the audience who wondered if this was somehow part of the act. A few long seconds later, we knew it was not and fast thinkers had already called for an ambulance. Much of the audience moved outside and watched as Tiny was lifted on a stretcher into the back of the ambulance. Ever the trooper, just before the doors closed, there was Tiny Tim blowing his trademark two-handed air kisses. We learned later that Tiny had suffered a heart attack and, while he recovered from it, he was advised to retire from performing. Sadly, he ignored that advice and died of a massive heart attack two months later at a gala benefit in Minneapolis while singing "Tiptoe Thru' the Tulips."

The author and Liz at the Ukulele Expo, 1996. (PHOTO BY MARVIN BELOFF)

Three years earlier, we had another Tiny Tim experience. In 1993, Liz and I had added antique malls to our list of places we haunted for uke-related treasures. In a glass case at the now long-gone Santa Monica Antique Market, we found a weird-looking Martin soprano ukulele with decals and paint splotches on it and the words "Miss Vicki" finger-painted on the sides. The description card said that the uke previously belonged to Tiny Tim and the price was $295, which was less than what a vintage Martin soprano might fetch without a celebrity connection. How could I refuse? After buying it, I contacted the dealer, Wes Parker, a former Los Angeles Dodger, who explained that he was given the uke by Tiny in 1970, in exchange for a baseball bat. While that all sounded reasonable (Tiny Tim was, in fact, a huge Los Angeles Dodgers fan), I knew I wouldn't be absolutely convinced until Tiny Tim himself confirmed the story.

Later that year, Tiny performed at a small Los Angeles club and we brought the uke with us. After the show, he stayed to greet fans and when our turn came, I showed him the Martin and repeated Wes Parker's account. He looked the uke over and said the story was just as I heard it. Then he signed it to "Mr. Jim." The story of the uke unintentionally grew a bit on January 17, 1994, at 4:31 a.m. That was the moment it flew off the shelf in Tommy Page's living room during the Northridge earthquake. Fortunately, the uke wasn't badly damaged, but we did apply a bit of "QuakeHOLD!" putty to it afterward.

The author with Tiny Tim in August 1993. (PHOTO BY ELIZABETH MAIHOCK BELOFF)

Tiny Tim's Martin ukulele. (PHOTO BY JOHN GIAMMATTEO)

Several articles in local papers appeared around the time of the Hall of Fame Expo. The idea of a group of ukulele enthusiasts traveling, in some cases long distances, to attend a daylong celebration of the instrument was a lively story and most of these articles included a prediction that the uke was coming back. A more comprehensive article by Michael Simmons appeared in the November 1996 issue of *Acoustic Guitar* magazine. The piece covered the basics of how the uke came to be, the two prior waves of popularity, the major Hawaiian and Mainland manufacturers, and short bios of Tiny Tim and Eddie Kamae, another legendary Hawaiian player. It was bullish about the future and included a sidebar of selected recordings and books. *Jim's Dog Has Fleas* was listed in the recordings along with albums by Cliff Edwards (Ukulele Ike) and Tiny Tim, and four of our books, *Favorites, Tips 'N' Tunes, Gems,* and *The Ukulele—A Visual History* ("forthcoming, December 1996") were joined by only one other title in the book section.

Our media exposure was also growing beyond just newspapers and magazines. On a trip back to New York, I was booked as a guest on *Breakfast Time* on the FX television channel with hosts Tom Bergeron and Laurie Hibberd. The show was an irreverent mix of interviews, information, and entertainment and had a puppet named Bob as a regular cast member. Again, a *Billboard* magazine executive pushing the return of the ukulele fit right in with the tone of the show, and I was invited on the program twice.

Ian Whitcomb also started to invite me onto his KPCC radio show out of Pasadena City College. Ian was sincerely enthusiastic about our efforts to promote the ukulele and, in turn, he was generous in helping to promote us. In addition, I was in conversation with Happy Traum about making a how-to-play video for his company, Homespun Tapes. Homespun specialized in music instruction videos and Happy was intrigued with the idea of one for the ukulele.

At the same time, I was toying with an even bigger idea: Quality ukuleles in music stores were hard to find. Kamaka was making around four thousand ukuleles a year, which were barely enough to satisfy the Hawaiian market. Music stores that wanted to bring in ukuleles were left with few options beyond inexpensive and poorly made imports. If someone asked me where they could find a decent ukulele, my standard answer was to go to a flea market or antique store or even to poke around in a grandparent's attic. Demand was increasingly there, but there was little supply. How could we help?

For a brief time, I looked into whether the molds for the famous "Islander" plastic uke designed by Mario Maccaferri were still available. Thanks to an unsolicited on-air comment from Arthur Godfrey, Maccaferri was overwhelmed with orders and went on to sell millions of the remarkably good-sounding and inexpensive ukes in the 1950s and '60s. Unfortunately, I was hearing that the molds had been sold years earlier and possibly melted down for scrap. At NAMM, the annual trade show for music stores, I even pled my case to Chris Martin of Martin Guitar that the time might be right to start making ukuleles again. I was unsuccessful.

In April 1997, Miller Freeman released *The Ukulele—A Visual History*. While they had their own in-house marketing and promotion department, they also hired an outside PR firm to generate additional interest. On June 17, I was back on NPR for "All Things Considered" to talk about the book. Rather than flying to Washington, D.C., Ray Suarez interviewed me remotely from a local NPR studio.

The reviews were very positive. Thanks to the eye-popping graphic design by Tommy Steele and Andy Engel, the "visual" part of the book received a lot of plaudits. The text was applauded, too, if for no other reason than that it was the first of its kind.

The Ukulele—A Visual History cover. (COURTESY OF BACKBEAT BOOKS, ROWMAN & LITTLEFIELD PUBLISHING GROUP, INC. AND GLOBE PEQUOT PRESS.)

Some reviews identified me as an editor of *Billboard* magazine, apparently ignoring my actual title in the press release and dismissing the idea that an ad sales executive could have written a book. Here are some selected quotes:

> "The text is dandy, and the pictures, snazzily laid out and all in color, of ukes, uke players, and uke paraphernalia, make this picture-on-every page album one of the most eyeballable (so to speak) books around."
> —*Booklist*

"*Billboard* editor Beloff offers an entertaining look at this whimsical, diminutive instrument. . . . Well written and enjoyable, this book will have library patrons tiptoeing through the tulips. The only book of its kind available, it is highly recommended."
—*Library Journal*

"Beloff, an associate editor of *Billboard* is obviously a uke nut."
—*San Francisco Examiner*

"With 112 pages and 200 color photos, this is a book that might make folks wonder, 'What took 'em so long?' Like the uke itself, Beloff's book is enjoyable . . . with more playful uke facts than have ever been crammed into one volume."
—*Honolulu Advertiser*

"All history should be this visual . . . this book is the Godiva chocolate of literary eye-candy."
—*Washington City Paper*

"The ukulele, the Rodney Dangerfield of four-stringed instruments, gets the respect it deserves in Jim Beloff's authoritative and entertaining volume."
—*Choate Rosemary Hall Alumni Magazine*

"Jim Beloff's book is a treasure for all uke lovers, especially 'ukeheads.'"
—*Pat Boone*

My two *Billboard* and ukulele lives intertwined again when *Billboard* Editor-in-Chief, Timothy White, gave the book a glowing review in the May 10 issue of *Billboard*. He described the book as an "eyewideningly handsome work with a splendidly fascinating text by Beloff, who is the nation's leading authority on the subject as well as the associate publisher of *Billboard*."

As wonderful as that review was, I can't help thinking now how it must have appeared to my superiors at *Billboard*. While I was as dedicated as ever to my job, it couldn't have escaped their notice that I was also finding the time to write a book. The ad sales department was always under pressure to deliver more pages and revenue and giving 100 percent was no longer enough. The expression "work hard, play hard" was popular at the time, but increasingly, I was expected to give more than 100 percent, and that seemed to tip the balance to just, work hard.

At the end of July, I had scheduled a short trip to Hawai'i for a couple of Borders bookstore signings, and some interviews and promotions surrounding Roy Sakuma's annual ukulele fest. Just before leaving for the airport, I had an uncomfortable phone call with Howard Lander. Even though I was owed the vacation time and had reserved the dates well in advance, he made me feel deeply guilty about jetting off to Hawai'i on behalf of my other life. That was the only trip I made to Hawai'i without Liz, and I arrived at the airport terribly confused about where my loyalties were and what I wanted to do with my life.

As fate would have it, there was a Hawaiian woman seated next to me during the flight that sensed the black cloud over my head. Her name was Pua Mahoe, a native Hawaiian elder (kupuna), teacher, and healer. And thanks to her gentle probing, by the time we arrived in Honolulu, I was beginning to sort out my priorities. One of them was that by 1997, I no longer related to many of the recordings on the *Billboard* album chart. Popular music was changing and, if anything, I was finding greater musical sustenance in the Great American Songbook songs that were tailor-made for the ukulele. Similarly, Liz was beginning to find her movie promotion assignments more and more about violence and guns. Our shorthand way of describing these films was "Die Hard 15." The truth was that we found greater satisfaction working on our own Flea Market Music projects, and, most importantly, they made people happy.

Another issue, oddly enough, had to do with golf. Over dinner one night, a long-time ally of mine in the corporate office confided that advancing beyond my current position would mean regularly socializing with top entertainment executives, and, as a result, I needed to become a decent golfer. I was not a natural when it came to most sports in general, and a laughably bad golfer on the few times I'd tried it. The company, my corporate friend said, was willing to subsidize my golf education, but I found the whole discussion depressing.

This led us both to think seriously about how we might sustain ourselves without the safety net of a regular paycheck and health care benefits. One factor in our favor was that we didn't have children and so we never had to worry about saving for college tuition and all the other expenses related to kids. Another was that we had just sold our loft in New York City, providing us with a temporary financial cushion.

By November I let Howard know of my desire to exit *Billboard*. At Howard's request, I stayed on for two more months and officially departed in late January 1998. Surprisingly, *Billboard* threw me a beautiful going-away lunch at a local restaurant, full of warm speeches and good wishes. Liz was invited, of course, but so was Ronny Schiff, which was a nice touch. In all, I had worked twenty years in the corporate magazine world. Ten years for Ziff-Davis, and another ten for *Billboard*. Now I would be working for myself.

And, I had three new projects very close to being released. Early in 1997, I happened to be seated next to Garson Foos, then vice president of Rhino Records, on a plane coming back from a record industry trade show. As it also happened, I had a prerelease copy of the uke history book with me. When I showed it to Garson, he got excited and immediately suggested that I produce a compilation CD of the great uke players for Rhino. At the time, Rhino was well known for its CD reissues, compilations, and elaborate box sets with clever titles and colorful graphics. Rhino had previously put out a disc titled, *Legends of Accordion*, and he thought a *Legends of Ukulele* would be a perfect follow-up.

Over at Homespun, Happy Traum had decided to move forward with my ukulele instructional video and he was set to tape it in Los Angeles at the end of January. Finally, I had started recording a new CD with musician/producer/engineer, Rick Cunha.

The day after the *Billboard* going-away party, I woke up to find myself in the ukulele business—full time.

Chapter 3

The Wave

King of All Media

These days, the NAMM (National Association of Music Merchants) trade show is held in Anaheim, California, at the end of January. With the holiday season over and a new year beginning, it's an ideal time for the music products industry to trade the winter cold for a few days of Disneyland fun and sun and do some business. In 1998, however, the show was temporarily moved to the Los Angeles Convention Center, which made it especially convenient for Liz and me. It was also perfectly timed for us as new full-time proprietors of Flea Market Music.

Our first task at NAMM was to meet with our partners at Hal Leonard. These were the early days of the Flea Market Music website, and we were exploring where to direct our online visitors interested in buying our books. We also proposed a new ukulele Christmas songbook, which we planned to have ready for the holiday selling season.

At NAMM, it's a sure bet that you'll run into noted musicians checking out the new products or demoing in the booths of companies whose instruments they play. One of the recognizable musicians to whom we talked was John Sebastian of Lovin' Spoonful fame. Not surprisingly, he was very approachable and happy to talk about ukuleles. It occurred to me that the Lovin' Spoonful hit "Daydream," with its classic shuffle feel, would be perfect on a uke, and we discussed the idea of someday including it in a book of more contemporary pop songs.

At the Homespun booth, we ran into guitar virtuoso Bob Brozman, who had made many videos for the company and was pleased to hear we were about to join the family. While there, we met with Homespun's founder, Happy Traum, about shooting the instructional portion of the video in a rented studio the following week. The video would start with me introducing the basic techniques, followed by teaching a half dozen easy to more challenging songs. He also gave a green light to open the video with a new original song, "I Don't Want to Say Aloha," which would be on the new CD I was recording with Rick Cunha. Happy would be directing the video and his advice was to sound unscripted, as if I were talking directly to the viewer. Oh, and another pro tip . . . make sure my fingernails were clean for the close-ups on my hands.

I also invited three guest players to be part of the video: Ian Whitcomb, Travis Harrelson, and Hawai'i-born Poncie Ponce. Poncie was best known for playing the uke-strumming cab driver, Kim, in the TV detective series, "Hawaiian Eye," that ran from 1959–1963. One of my colleagues at *Billboard* was Poncie's son-in-law and he helped make the introduction. A natural entertainer, Poncie eventually developed a nightclub act that showcased his uke skills. One of the highlights was his instrumental arrangement of "The Stars and Stripes Forever" on the ukulele. It was a wonderful bit of virtuosity and Poncie would end it with a mini-American flag popping up from behind his Martin tenor. He performed this arrangement on the video and then revealed the small lever installed on the back of his uke to pop the flag. Ever the showbiz veteran, Poncie admitted with a smile that it was "a little bit flashy."

My two other guests on the video, Ian and Travis, showed off their own unique styles. Travis demonstrated his jaw-dropping right-hand strums while sharing playing tips on "Five Foot Two, Eyes of Blue" and "Tea for Two." He also had advice for avoiding what he called an "Excedrin headache" by breaking down complicated techniques into more manageable pieces. Ian was charming as always and performed the old Al Jolson novelty song, "Where Did Robinson Crusoe Go with Friday on Saturday Night?" In his introduction to the song, Ian recounted the story of recording the song in 1966 and how it "bubbled up" to 101 on the *Billboard* Hot 100 chart.

In the final segment of the video, I talked briefly about the history of the ukulele and presented some favorite examples from our personal collection. This included vintage ukes made by historic manufacturers like Martin, National, and the early Hawaiian makers, as well as more colorful ones with fun graphics and names. The setting for that portion of the video was the house we bought after living at Tommy Page's for three years. A classic 1950s-era mid-century modern in the Hollywood Hills, the house featured a flat roof, terrazzo floors, a large deck and pool, and floor-to-ceiling

Right: *The Joy of Uke 1.*
(COURTESY OF HOMESPUN
VIDEO)

Below: The author with
Poncie Ponce during
the taping of *The Joy
of Uke 1.* (PHOTO BY
ELIZABETH MAIHOCK
BELOFF)

windows overlooking Universal Studios and the San Fernando Valley. The house's previous owner had been entertainment legend and talk-show host, Merv Griffin, who had bought it for his son, Tony. A condition of the contract was that, at the closing, we would get a signed photo from Merv that said, "mi casa es su casa" ("my house is your house"). Perhaps they thought we were kidding, but there was no photo at the closing. We reminded our brokers that this was no joke and, not long after, they hand-delivered the photo, which we gave pride-of-place to in our front hall.

The Rhino *Legends of Ukulele* CD was also moving along. As compilation producer, my job was to pull together a list of preferred artists and tracks, write the liner notes, and work with the designer on the cover art. The task of recommending the artist and track list was complicated by the fact that some of the tracks were quite old and the master recordings were either missing or lost, or the tracks that were current were not licensable. One of the recordings at the top of my wish list was Iz's "Over the Rainbow/What a Wonderful World" medley. Unfortunately, Iz's family had the final say on licensing this track and despite our pleas, we were turned down. We also encountered availability issues on older recordings like Cliff "Ukulele Ike" Edwards's "Singing in the Rain." In that case, we had better luck with his 1928 Columbia single "That's My Weakness Now." To many, Cliff Edwards will always be remembered as the voice of Jiminy Cricket, in Disney's animated film, *Pinocchio*. He also sang "When You Wish Upon a Star," for the film. For the compilation, though, the track we selected needed to feature him playing the ukulele. We hit another roadblock with the Roy Smeck–penned instrumental "Ukulele Bounce" and so we replaced it with "Uke Said It," another Smeck original. Despite its polarizing reputation, I knew we had to include Tiny Tim's biggest hit, "Tiptoe Thru' the Tulips," which appeared on his best-selling album *God Bless Tiny Tim*. In researching "Tiptoe," I met with the legendary producer of the album, Richard Perry, who revealed that Tiny didn't play the ukulele on the recording.

The eighteen tracks we ended up with were balanced between recordings by long-gone historic players like Johnny Marvin, King Benny Nawahi, Cliff Edwards, and beloved British banjo-uke entertainer George Formby, and more current practitioners like Ian Whitcomb, The Ukulele Orchestra of Great Britain, and the Ka'au Crater Boys led by Hawaiian uke phenom Troy Fernandez. Once again, I volunteered a song of my own, the title track from my upcoming solo CD, *For the Love of Uke*, which featured a uke solo by Lyle Ritz. Lyle closed out the *Legends* CD with his 1995 recording of "Lulu's Back in Town" from his *Time* CD on Roy Sakuma's record label.

I had an especially good time working on the cover design with Rhino art director, Hugh Brown. Hugh had an open and playful attitude toward this project and featured our more colorful novelty instruments (like the "Betty Boop" and "Jungle" uke) and hula nodders on the cover. Along the hinge of the jewel case, he placed a ukulele fretboard, and behind the CD, he placed vintage translucent ukulele string packets. The twenty-page booklet included my track notes, plus a brief history of the ukulele. Garson Foos, cofounder of Rhino, wrote the cheeky introduction. Here's a sample:

> After the tremendous success of our *Legends of Accordion* collection (recently certified Tin—over 5,000 units sold), we were searching for the perfect follow-up. Enter Jim Beloff—not your ordinary advertising sales bigwig. First of all, he's almost as interested in talking music as he is in selling advertising. Secondly, if he's not talking about Todd Rundgren B-sides, he's preaching ukulele like a TV evangelist without the southern accent.
>
> Flying back from somewhere several years ago, Jim and I happened to be on an empty plane together. Jim had just received the first designed draft of his incredible ukulele book *The Ukulele—A Visual History*. I was floored. . . . I became convinced *Legends of Ukulele* was an album we had to produce."

I started my liner notes with: "'Uke can't be serious!' Who would have thought that a musical instrument so humble and informal could inspire a recording with a title like *Legends of Ukulele?*" Clearly, the uke was still having respectability issues. I note, too, the first appearance of the phrase "uke can't be serious," which would be recycled a year later as the title of my first concerto for ukulele and orchestra.

There was also a timing consideration with the *Legends* CD. I was pushing to have it be released by early July, so I could promote it on a trip to Hawai'i at the end of the month. I had tracked down a couple of the more senior Hawaiian virtuosos featured on the CD, like Nelson Waikiki and Eddie Bush, and was hoping to feature them at some of the planned Borders bookstore events. Lyle had already signed on. In February, however, Rhino had still not cleared four of the tracks.

In early March, Liz and I flew back East. The primary purpose was to meet with Maria Maccaferri, the widow of Mario Maccaferri who had designed and manufactured the hugely successful line of "Islander" plastic ukuleles. Maria was almost twenty years younger than Mario, and, in 1998, she was still running The French American Reed Mfg. Co., the company that she and Mario established in 1939 in Paris, France. We met her at the Mount Vernon, New York, factory where the saxophone and clarinet reeds were manufactured.

Joining us for the meeting was my sister Phyllis's husband, Dale Webb, who had a background in mechanical engineering. At the time, Dale was working in product design and manufacturing, but he had taken an interest in my pursuit of a good quality, affordable ukulele. At the very least, I hoped that Dale might be inspired by meeting Maria. As it turns out, Maria could not have been more welcoming. She was happy to share her memories of the peak Islander years when the factory had three hundred employees, many of them women. She also confirmed that the ukulele molds had been sold and were no longer available.

The author with Maria Maccaferri in 1998. (PHOTO BY ELIZABETH MAIHOCK BELOFF)

Originally, Mario's plastic ukulele was supposed to be a trial run for his greatest ambition, an all-plastic guitar. That all changed when the uke took off, but he still had had great hopes for his guitar. Mario did eventually make and sell an all-plastic guitar, but it was nowhere near the success of the ukulele. Maria still had the molds for the guitar, but nobody seemed to want them.

As we were leaving, Maria gave Dale the original carved wood model for the Islander, which was itself based on a Martin soprano uke. She also gave Liz and me an Islander uke that was hand-painted on the front by Carrie Singhi. Carrie was the sister of May Singhi Breen, who from the 1920s on, was one of the most successful ukulele

Left: The Maccaferri "Islander" model. (PHOTO BY HARRY LEVENSTEIN)

Right: "Islander" ukulele hand-painted by Carrie Singhi. (PHOTO BY JOHN GIAMMATTEO)

popularizers and songbook publishers. Known as "The Original Ukulele Lady," May was responsible for convincing publishers to add ukulele chord grids to their sheet music. Carrie, May, and May's husband, songwriter Peter DeRose ("Deep Purple"), were all personal friends of Maria and Mario. Liz, Dale, and I left the meeting eager to explore our next steps.

Ten days later, back in Los Angeles, Rick Cunha and I mastered my new solo CD, *For the Love of Uke*. Once again, Ronny was responsible for my meeting Rick, whose grandfather was legendary Hawaiian singer and songwriter, Sonny Cunha. In fact, the first time I met Rick was to learn more about Sonny and ask if I could include his photo of Sonny playing a ukulele in my history book. Sonny's greatest contribution to Hawaiian music was the popularizing of *hapa haole* (literal translation "half white") songs like "My Honolulu Hula Girl," which were a blend of Hawaiian and Tin Pan Alley influences. Rick, too, was a well-known musician and a founding member of the 1960's California folk-rock group, Hearts & Flowers, a band that later included Bernie Leadon who would go on to be a founding member of the Eagles.

Rick had built a recording studio in his home garage in Van Nuys and by the time we first met in 1997, I had accumulated enough new songs that I was ready to make a new CD. One of those songs was "Charles Ives," a tribute to the twentieth-century American composer. The music Ives wrote was too modern for most early 1900s audiences, and he often had to pay orchestras to play his compositions. My fascination with Ives was due to his being one of the most successful artists who also had a day job. In addition to his composing life, Ives co-owned a highly respected New York City insurance company, where he pioneered the art of selling life insurance. Because I found myself torn between a full-time sales job and music-related projects, Ives became an inspiration to me, and I wrote a song about him. The first verse was:

He was a man who sold insurance,
He was a man who wrote a symphony,
He was a man who led two lives.
When I get thinking that I cannot do it all,
Then I remember, Charles Ives.

After hearing the new songs, and especially, "Charles Ives," Rick agreed to produce my new CD. Recording sessions began in 1997, and unlike, my first album, Rick brought in some ace studio musicians to help flesh out the songs. One of the most acclaimed was Hal Blaine, the celebrated drummer of the Los Angeles studio band, the Wrecking Crew. Although the Wrecking Crew days were long past, Hal was still active as a studio drummer and he was always happy to sit in on Rick's sessions. He also got a kick out of knowing that I was in touch with Lyle Ritz, his bandmate and good friend from the Wrecking Crew days. In fact, Lyle participated in the album, too, with his soloing on the title song, "For the Love of Uke." Because he was in Hawai'i, we sent Lyle the recording of the song with me on uke and vocals and Simeon Pillich on acoustic bass. Lyle then took that into a studio in Honolulu and recorded his part over it. He then sent that part back and we added it to the existing track. I was thrilled.

The album also included my songs, "Shakeytown," written after the Northridge earthquake, "I Don't Want to Say Aloha," a Hawaiian love song, and "Old Sheet Music Moon," inspired by a comment overheard at an Ian Whitcomb outdoor concert. "Hannah &" was a song written for my late grandmother. After her husband, Phil, had passed away, Hannah added an ampersand to her signature on all of her personal correspondence and note cards. Rick wrote cello and bass parts for "Charles Ives," and I also recorded four instrumentals, including chord solo covers of "'Til There Was You," "When You Wish Upon a Star," and "Lucy & Fred," which was a medley of the "I Love Lucy" and the "Flintstones" TV theme songs. The other instrumental was my salute to Lyle, titled "Lyle's Smiles." That track included Simeon Pillich on acoustic bass, Hal Blaine on drums, and Rick Cunha with a swinging Gretsch guitar solo. Later on, "Lyle's Smiles" ended up on another ukulele compilation CD, which led to inclusion on an early Spotify playlist, which then led to dozens of other Spotify listener playlists. As of 2020, it has been streamed over four million times.

Along with all of these other projects, Liz and I were assembling our next songbook, *Jumpin' Jim's Ukulele Christmas*. Every year, Christmas songbooks were a big seller for Hal Leonard, and now that we had proved there was a market for ukulele songbooks, a collection filled with classic Christmas songs and carols made good sense. Because so many of the best-loved carols and songs were in the public domain, we decided to fill the book with only public domain standards, plus a couple of my originals. Ultimately, we settled on thirty arrangements, including "Deck the Halls," "Hark, the Herald Angels Sing," "Jingle Bells," "Joy to the World," and, of course, "Silent Night." Like everyone, we had great affection for these timeless melodies and the idea of making them available to the ukulele community was exciting.

The Christmas songbook was special to us for another, more personal reason. Both of us were Christmas babies. I was born on December 25 and Liz's birthday was two days before, on the twenty-third. I grew up with people feeling sorry for me, certain that I must get cheated out of presents. I had a pretty good comeback though. . . . I was Jewish. And yet, they were sort of right. Our family tried Hanukkah a few times but eventually decided that exchanging all our gifts with each other on the twenty-fifth was more fun. I never did feel cheated, though. I loved having my birthday on such a happy and celebrated day. And I loved the fact that it was so connected to music. My mother has a memory of carolers singing in the hospital the day I was born.

My Christmas birthday became the inspiration for one of the original songs in the book titled, "When You're Born on Christmas Day." The other original, "The Last House," was inspired by the slow and steady removal of outdoor Christmas lights after the holidays and cheering on the one house that resists taking them down the longest.

For this songbook, my cover credit was "compiled and arranged." Beyond pulling together a list of carols and songs to be considered, I also selected the keys and chords with ukulele players specifically in mind. Like the *Tips 'N' Tunes* book, some arrangements included "parenthetical chords," which could be ignored or played depending on the player's skill. One piece of music I especially enjoyed arranging was a chord solo of Tchaikovsky's "Dance of the Sugar-Plum Fairy." It was another example of how a complex piece of music could be "reduced," and yet still retain the essential melody and harmony.

Liz had fun with the graphic design, putting the uke on the front cover in a halo surrounded by stylized snowflakes and putting my floating head in a Christmas ornament on the back. Inside, she filled the empty spaces at the end of some songs with vintage Christmas cards she found at paper shows and flea markets. From what we

Jumpin' Jim's Ukulele Christmas cover (COURTESY OF FLEA MARKET MUSIC, INC.)

could tell, utilizing the available "negative" or empty space in a songbook this way was something novel, and from then on, we took advantage of these blank spots to make the books more personal and unique.

Nineteen-ninety-eight was also the year we created an online home for Flea Market Music. My dad knew of a young company in Meriden that was designing websites and after an initial meeting with Web Solutions, we decided to take the plunge. Led by co-owner and programmer Tom Barton, Web Solutions took our input and customized a site specifically designed to foster a digital ukulele community. At first, this included a chat room and guestbook and a "Bulletin Board" where players could leave ukulele-related postings. Visitors could also view and read about our books and CDs, but because we weren't set up to sell directly from the site, we provided phone numbers of retailers and distributors from whom they could purchase the products.

These were the early days of the internet when we were all trying to figure out the best ways to take advantage of this new medium. It occurred to me that one of the biggest challenges was how to keep the site fresh so that guests would want to visit frequently. My first impulse was to provide the new content myself, perhaps via regularly updated postings on the home page. Thinking it through, though, I knew that eventually this would become a chore. It then dawned on me that the visitors themselves were creating their own continuously changing content. The Bulletin Board, in particular, started attracting uke fans, artists, and businesses that were constantly posting to each other. Another continuously changing page was the Marketplace, where folks could buy and sell ukuleles and related products. To protect ourselves from liability, we placed a disclaimer at the bottom of the Marketplace that cleared Flea Market Music of all responsibility regarding the transactions.

Perhaps the most important page was the Player Directory. Right from the outset, we recognized that uke enthusiasts were eager to meet and play with other enthusiasts. Web Solutions designed a very simple interface for visitors to register on the site by state and city and even by country. This meant, for example, that a registered player in Chicago could email another registered player in Chicago about jamming together or even starting a ukulele club.

FLEA MARKET MUSIC, INC.

Welcome to Flea Market Music!

JIM BELOFF

Home

On-line Store

Calendar

Flashbacks

Mailing List

Chat Room

Add a Link

Guestbook

Marketplace

Bulletin Board

Collector's Uke Yak

E-Tuner

Finding a ukulele at a local flea market in 1992 changed my life. Not only did I find my musical soul mate, but it also inspired me to share the joy of the ukulele with others. Here you'll find information on Jumpin' Jim's ukulele songbooks and all other books, Cds, videos and the Fluke ukulele. Because one of our main goals is to build an on-line community for ukulele players, we have developed several interactive areas. The Bulletin Board is a place to post messages about a variety of topics, Add a Link is for connecting to other uke-related sites, the Chat Room is for real time communication and Chuck "Frets" Fayne answers your questions regarding vintage ukes on the Collector's Uke Yak. We'd love to hear from you, so please feel free to comment in our Guestbook, and don't forget to leave your name and address for our Mailing List. Stay tuned to this site for future ukulele related products.

STAY TUNED-NOVEMBER 4, 2000!!

The new MDHF catalogue is in the mail now! This is a good time to make sure we have your street address so you can get a copy. All the new products have been added to our online store and a few of our most exciting new CDs are pictured below. Just click and order directly. We also have a neat new ukulele wooden puzzle in the UKEmporium section where you'll also find all the uke videos including an introductory one for kids ages 5-11.

www.fleamarketmusic.com home page in 2000. (COURTESY OF FLEA MARKET MUSIC, INC.)

At the end of April, we flew back to the East Coast for Liz's parents' fiftieth-anniversary party. Since we were already that far east, we decided to fly a bit further and spend a week in London. While there, we checked off several must-see tourist destinations and also dropped in on a couple of well-known music stores, where I was happy to find our books in stock.

The high point of the trip was an evening spent in a pub with the Ukulele Orchestra of Great Britain. The UOGB was a group of very talented and dry-witted musicians who took great pleasure in performing material not normally associated with the ukulele. Everything from rock songs like the Talking Heads "Psycho Killer," to the theme songs from *Shaft* and *The Good, the Bad and the Ugly*. I had been in touch with UOGB founder, George Hinchliffe, while compiling tracks for the Rhino CD

The author with the Ukulele Orchestra of Great Britain in 1998. (PHOTO BY ELIZABETH MAIHOCK BELOFF)

and mentioned that we might be traveling to London. Once there, we arranged to meet in an upstairs room at the Empress of Russia Pub in Islington. Six members of the group turned out and I remember we performed for each other all night. In my journal, I wrote that they played Joni Mitchell's "A Case of You," Nirvana's "Smells Like Teen Spirit," three songs with "wild" in the title — "Running Wild," "Wild Thing," and "Born to Be Wild" and the song I put on the Rhino CD, "Johnny B. Goode." We also established ties with UOGB member Peter Brooke Turner, who would visit us in Los Angeles in the future.

As the saying goes, "when it rains, it pours." On top of managing all of these projects in various stages of completion, I received a call from my Choate advisor, Phil Ventre. In addition to conducting the Choate student orchestra, Phil was also the founder and conductor of the Wallingford Symphony Orchestra, a full-sized professional group that used the Paul Mellon Arts Center as their home venue. Phil had been a mentor to me during my two years at Choate and was also the music director of my bicentennial musical, *Two Sides of Heaven*. We had stayed in touch through the years, and he had followed our ukulele adventures with interest. During a wide-ranging phone call, I mentioned that, as far I knew, there had never been a concerto for solo ukulele and symphony orchestra. Without skipping a beat, Phil said, "Let's do it. You compose it, and the Wallingford Symphony will perform it with you as the guest artist." Never mind that I had never written anything for an orchestra and knew nothing about arranging for the various instruments. Oh, and he wanted it to premiere in the fall of 1999, the following year.

The Wave Begins

I released my solo CD, *For the Love of Uke*, in May on our Flea Market Music label. Because ukulele-based albums were still a novelty, I was able to find a couple of companies to help distribute the CD. It also received some positive notices:

"On this release, Beloff shines on all fronts, from his charming, original compositions (notably, the title track, 'Hannah &,' 'Charles Ives,' and 'Big in Japan') to his instrumental interpretations. . . . As an instrumentalist, Beloff coaxes warm, rich tones from his tenor and soprano ukes, and as a vocalist, he comes across with the supple grace of James Taylor."
—*Billboard*

"Beloff seems to be on a one-man mission to popularize the ukulele, or at least bring some respectability to the neglected instrument. After writing a wonderful book as a tribute to the instrument, he has now released his second album. In his vocal and songwriting styles, Beloff is comparable to Michael Franks, and he is presented to good advantage, thanks to Rick Cunha's understated production. Beloff's songs are just quirky enough to work. . . . The ukulele is a modest little instrument deserving of wider popularity. This latest release, like Beloff's book, should push that cause forward."
—Dirty Linen

For the Love of Uke CD cover. (COURTESY OF FLEA MARKET MUSIC, INC.)

Two weeks before our trip to Hawai'i, Rhino released *Legends of Ukulele*. True to form, Rhino had fun with the press release, warning record stores in the headline: "Don't Nuke the Uke as It Tiptoes into Stores on July 14." The rest of the release was in the same vein with "The follow-up to the remarkably unsuccessful *Legends of Accordion*" and "Proof that size doesn't matter, the ukulele has been the medium for virtuoso performances for more than seventy years. Of course, Tiny Tim's 'Tiptoe Thru' the Tulips with Me,' is here—surely the 'Stairway to Heaven' of ukulele music."

The *Legends* CD received lots of reviews. Here are a few colorful quotes:

"This collection is proof positive that ukuleles are cool, no matter what you think of Tiny Tim."
—*Audio*

"It's hard to believe, looking at this homely little instrument, but once upon a time, the ukulele ruled. . . . This disc has plenty to argue its case, from virtuoso jazz to humble folk to aromatic old chestnuts such as 'Do I Love You? Yes I Do!' Skip the obligatory Tiny Tim track and go right to the ineffable Ohta San and 'Little Grass Shack.' The production and selection are impeccable, and the way over-researched liner notes are from Jim Beloff author of *The Ukulele—A Visual History* and contributor of the noirishly cute 'For the Love of Uke.'"
—*Variety* (Grade B+)

"Who knew you could do all that with a ukulele?"
—*Modern Lounge*

"*Legends of Ukulele* brings us 18 tracks of pure tropical mojo. *Legends*—producer Jim Beloff could have easily tanked this disc. But, to his credit, he's gathered a skillful range of uke pedagogy. On the whole, a near-perfect on all scales."
—*Fine Arts Guild*

"Lovingly assembled by Jim Beloff, former Associate Publisher of *Billboard* magazine and now guru of the late 20th century uke renaissance, this collection brings together an impressive variety of styles, genres and techniques."
—*Cool and Strange Music Magazine*

" . . . an hour of pure fun."
—*Scripps Howard News Service*

". . . only an intractable grouch could fail to be charmed by this goofy roundup."
—*Guitar Player*

". . . with Tiny out of the way after the second track, the laughter turns to respectful silence and then admiration, if not awe. Intelligently programmed and annotated, *Legends of Ukulele* should be required listening for anyone who dismisses the instrument as a dime-store toy."
—*Newsday*

"My favorite track is Tiny Tim's 'Tiptoe Thru' the Tulips.' This Top-10 single was dismissed as camp when it first came out, but in hindsight it is a glorious record, Tiny's falsetto soaring beautifully over the lush, old-fashioned melody."
—*The Sunday Star-Ledger*

". . . notorious catalog-filler Rhino Records is giving the ukulele a new day in the sun (and not just in Hawai'i). In featuring so many artists and genres, this disc reveals hitherto undiscovered elements of this tiny tune-maker."
—*Boston Globe*

"What a pleasure it is—I couldn't even make it through the whole CD during a first listen without grabbing my own uke and having a frenzied solo jam session. Uke gotta get it."
—*San Francisco Bay Guardian*

"Once you own this collection, you won't know how you've lived without it."
—*Honolulu Magazine*

Later that month, in Hawai'i, we set up three Borders bookstore promotions tied to the Rhino release. At each stop, I had one of the "legends" from the CD, Nelson Waikiki, Eddie Bush, and Lyle Ritz. While there, we did radio interviews and

Legends of Ukulele CD. (COURTESY OF RHINO ENTERTAINMENT COMPANY)

other promotional work as well as visit music stores. The consensus was that sales of ukuleles were better than ever. Ukulele House, a big, beautiful store in the open-air Royal Hawaiian Center in Waikiki, had just opened three months earlier and was focusing solely on ukuleles and related products. We also talked to the Langley Ukulele Ensemble (LUE) at the invitation of their energetic director, Peter Luongo. The group—made up of students and young adults from Langley, British Columbia—was in Hawai'i to perform at Roy Sakuma's annual festival. All through the week, you would find the LUE playing around Waikiki. Their singing and, especially their playing, was extremely precise and even their movements were choreographed. Peter asked

The author with Eddie Bush in Honolulu, Hawai'i, 1998. (PHOTO BY ELIZABETH MAIHOCK BELOFF)

Liz and me to meet the group in his hotel room one evening to share our story and thoughts about the future of the instrument.

Earlier that year I had met with a couple of public relations agencies. Now that we were full time in the uke business, I thought we should at least look into hiring professionals to help us promote our story. I remember one meeting where the press agent offered to give us a special deal of only $3,000 per month (regularly $5,000) to represent us. I swallowed hard and asked what we might expect in return for that kind of investment. The answer was that they couldn't promise anything. All they could do was try to generate some interest.

There was no way we were in a position to cover that kind of monthly expense. The good news was that we never had to. Until that moment, we'd done pretty well with publicity, but the one-two punch of the ukulele history book and the Rhino compilation took it to another level. On Saturday, July 4, my third NPR interview aired, this time with Scott Simon for "Weekend Edition." The title of the interview was "The Immortal Ukulele" and the focus was the new Rhino compilation. Rhino's promotion department set this up, but something else seemed to be at play. It turned out that the return of the ukulele was a good story. I'm not sure who coined the term "third wave" of ukulele popularity. But, between Iz's global hit with "Over the Rainbow/What a Wonderful World," George Harrison's and Paul McCartney's public embrace of the instrument, and the books and CDs we were pumping out, there was this sense that interest in the ukulele was growing again. It was considered the third wave because of the two prior ones: the first during the late teens and 1920s when vaudeville met the Jazz Age, and the second during the postwar 1950s, fueled by the media saturation of uke lover Arthur Godfrey and returning servicemen who had sampled Hawaiian culture while in the Pacific.

I had yet another theory for this new interest. In the late 1990s, computers and the internet were taking up a growing percentage of work and personal time. It seemed as if we were living more and more in a digital, plugged-in world. In fact, I noticed some of the earliest and most enthusiastic advocates for the instrument were computer programmers. My gut was telling me that because of all the time spent logged on, an easy-to-learn, portable musical instrument that didn't require electricity was suddenly a fresh idea. Plus, the music most associated with the instrument was delightfully retro, melodic, and especially fun to sing and play with others. With apologies to Club Med, the ukulele was becoming the musical antidote to civilization.

On August 2, the *Los Angeles Times* published a major story by Lynne Heffley on the reemergence of the ukulele, headlined, "Still Small, but Making a Big Comeback." Until then, the press we received revolved around a particular book or CD release. This article, too, was in response to the Rhino compilation, but the story angle was much wider than any one product. First, the author bookended the piece with her own personal, family history with the ukulele. She also covered the growth of internet-based uke sites, interviewed other players represented on the Rhino CD, and, finally, she drilled down a bit on "why" this might be happening now. Here is what I said:

> I think it's connected to the fact that, at one time or another in the past, the uke was part of the musical center of some kind of occasion that was happy, when a bunch of people were all singing together. Maybe there's some desire in us, in the uncertainty of life these days, to remember and re-create moments like that.

Less than a week later, we celebrated the release of the Rhino CD with a sold-out concert at McCabe's Guitar Shop, a historic, acoustic instrument music retailer and venue in Santa Monica. The idea behind the concert was to perform as many of the songs from the Rhino disc as possible. Liz and I were the hosts of the evening and some of the featured artists included Ian and Regina Whitcomb, Joel Eckhaus (who flew in from Portland, Maine), Fred Sokolow, Rick Cunha, Shep Stern, Janet Klein, and John Zhender, the head of McCabe's repair department, who had an especially deep affection for the uke. The show was a big success, so big, in fact, that the audience and players all wanted to know when the next concert was. I also noticed something else that I filed away for the future—many of the audience members had brought their ukuleles with them to the show.

Four days after the McCabe's concert, another major article about the ukulele appeared in the *San Francisco Bay Guardian* titled "A Movement in Four Strings." With the subtitle, "The Little Ukulele Is Back and Getting Bigger," this was another wide-angle piece that covered the past, present, and future with quotes from me, Roy Sakuma, and David Hurd, a maker of high-end ukuleles on the Big Island of Hawai'i. The article also paid tribute to Israel Kamakawiwo'ole, who had passed away the year before at the age of thirty-eight, and acknowledged the uke virtuosity of Troy Fernandez of the Ka'au Crater Boys as having inspired a new generation of Hawaiian players. Both Roy Sakuma and David Hurd reported that business was booming. In particular, Roy, said, "with all the kids playing today, there's no telling how far this could go." This is a bit of what I had to say:

Like a lot of people who grew up in the '60s and '70s, I was a big fan of the guitar and played it for thirty years. But within two weeks (of discovering the Martin), I had stopped playing the guitar entirely. I was struck immediately by two things: the 'ukulele was far more portable, so if I traveled, I could take it with me. The second thing was that I wasn't giving up anything by giving up two strings. In fact, it was more of a challenge to make out of four strings what I could out of six strings. I love my guitar, but it mostly collects dust.

By now my Homespun video, *The Joy of Uke*, had been released and received good notices. *Vintage Guitar* ended their review with, "Who knows, we may be in the midst of a uke renaissance!" Homespun, like Flea Market Music, had distribution through Hal Leonard, and soon the video was available in music stores. One person who bought it was movie actor Sam Neill (of *Jurassic Park* fame). Sam's assistant tracked me down in Los Angeles and asked if I gave private lessons. I didn't—but for Sam, I did! At that point, he had been playing for three weeks and been working through my video

The author with Sam Neill. (PHOTO BY ELIZABETH MAIHOCK BELOFF)

and *Tips 'N' Tunes* method book. His sudden interest was due to shooting a film in Hawai'i titled *Molokai: The Story of Father Damien*, about the Belgian priest who worked at the leper colony on the Hawaiian island of Moloka'i. Sam came to our house in mid-August, and several times afterward, whenever he was in Los Angeles. Thoughtful and unpretentious, Sam was serious about improving his technique and took a real interest in our upcoming projects. He was especially keen on our publishing a songbook of more contemporary pop songs and Beatles tunes.

Rounding into the fall of 1998, it seemed like everything was happening at once. The Ukulele Hall of Fame Museum had booked me to perform and emcee a four-stop "Ukulele Masters" tour in early October. Lyle Ritz, Byron Yasui, Led Kaapana, Bob Brozman, Joel Eckhaus, and I were packaged as an "opportunity to hear the finest expressions of ukulele music on the planet." The tour would start at Symphony Space in New York City, then travel on to Sage Hall at Smith College in Northampton, Massachusetts, Paine Hall at Harvard University in Cambridge, and finish at the State Street Church in Portland, Maine.

Before that, I flew to San Francisco for the weekend to do a radio interview at KALX in Berkeley and then play on the same bill with the ukulele punk duo, Pineapple Princess, at Club Cocodrie, a North Beach bar. Pineapple Princess was made up of Beth Allen and Pamela Schulting, who mixed screaming punk tunes with traditional Hawaiian songs. One of their songs was "We Suck," and their motto was "Uke til ya puke." Beth had invited me to perform with them and despite the big difference in our musical styles, she was a big supporter of our books and CDs. Steven Strauss, a wonderful local bass player and uke player I'd worked with before, backed me up for the gig, but the sound system was lacking, and nobody seemed to be listening. On the return flight to Burbank, I spoke with singer-songwriter Tracy Chapman, who noticed I was wearing a uke-themed T-shirt and carrying a ukulele. I had read that her first instrument was a ukulele and I said I hoped it was true since I mentioned it in my history book. She said it was, and I gave her a copy.

We also had a couple of songbook irons in the fire. With the *Ukulele Christmas* book out and in stores for preholiday sales, we turned our attention to two new themed songbooks. One was a long-considered collection of '60s pop songs that we would title *Jumpin' Jim's '60s Uke-In*, and the other was a collection of well-known Hawaiian and *hapa haole* songs that would become *Jumpin' Jim's Gone Hawaiian*.

Liz and I flew to the East Coast a few days before the "Ukulele Masters" tour began. I had set up a meeting with Martin Guitar in Nazareth, Pennsylvania, to explore the possibility of collaborating in some way on a line of ukuleles. My brother-in-law, Dale, joined me. The three-and-a-half-hour meeting included a tour of the factory. It was fascinating, especially for Dale, who was an avid woodworker. We were both struck by how open Martin was in sharing some of their manufacturing techniques. That was not at all typical in the industry where Dale was currently working. At the time, Martin was building the "Backpacker" ukulele in their Mexico facility. With its narrow-waisted design, the Backpacker uke was inspired by the slimmed-down Backpacker guitar, which was promoted as a more travel-friendly alternative. The Backpacker uke, however, seemed to beg the question of why anyone needed a more portable version of an already portable instrument. Although we never did work directly with Martin, we did learn that the fretted-instrument world was a friendly place that welcomed and encouraged outsiders.

If only for the title, the "Ukulele Masters" tour was a success. For those who merely knew the uke as a prop for a backyard luau, the combination of the two words "ukulele" and "masters" was a delicious challenge to the existing order of things. The tour really did live up to its title. Among those in the know, Lyle's reputation preceded him, but Byron Yasui, also an accomplished multi-instrumentalist, was equally at home on jazz double bass, classical and jazz guitar, and ukulele. In addition, Byron was a longtime professor of music theory and composition at the University of Hawai'i and an award-winning composer of serious music. Both he and Lyle performed regularly in Hawai'i as the bass/uke duo "Ukulele Madness."

Bob Brozman from Northern California and Led Kaapana from Hawai'i were also virtuosos on several instruments. Originally from the Big Island of Hawai'i, Led was renowned as a slack key guitarist and master of the ukulele and bass, and Brozman was the "King of the National Guitar" and a member of the "Cheap Suit Serenaders," led by cartoonist and banjo player, Robert Crumb. Joel Eckhaus had studied the ukulele with "Wizard of the Strings," Roy Smeck, and had mastered several challenging Smeck original instrumentals. He also was an experienced luthier and had built the ukulele that he played on the tour. Oh, and Joel also played the saw.

In my role as Master of Ceremonies, I played a handful of my own songs. Early in the show, however, I said this, "If you play the ukulele, at some point you may have to wrestle with this next song. This is how I've chosen to deal with it." I then started playing and singing a smooth jazz version of "Tiptoe Thru' the Tulips" on my tenor uke. Joel was also on the stage with me and during the solo section, he pulled out his saw from its case and with a bow began to simulate the high Tiny Tim falsetto. The audience had a good laugh at that and at the end of the solo, after acknowledging Joel, I would say, "By the way, if you're wondering, it's a Stanley."

After the first concert in New York City, we went down to ABC headquarters to tape a segment with Barry Mitchell, for his late-night "World News Now" comedy show. Time was tight, but he managed to give each of us our moment, including a brief Q and A with tour producer and Ukulele Hall of Fame Museum director, Paul Syphers. We started the segment by plucking the memorable four-note theme music used at the top of the ABC *World News Tonight* broadcast and we closed with Joel's and my version of "Tiptoe" with the rest of the "Masters" jamming along.

The comeback of the ukulele story kept spreading. The *Boston Globe* did an article tied to the Ukulele Masters tour titled, "Nowhere to Go but Up: The New Golden Age of the Ukulele." They interviewed Paul Syphers and me. When it was suggested that Paul's ukulele obsession is odd, insane, even, he laughs and says, "You can't insult a ukulele player." Later on, I came to his defense saying, "The expectations are so deliciously low for all of us that it's only up from here." When pressed on why the ukulele was getting popular now, Paul had a wonderful response, referring to it as "a kind of alternative portable radio. You can make your music on the go." My response was, "Things have cycles, and I think people are once again appreciating the craft and joy of the songs from the Tin Pan Alley period in the '20s and '30s. People forget that for two periods in the twentieth century, the uke wasn't just popular, it was *wildly* popular. If you ask people over a certain age, it's like, 'Of course I had a uke—everyone had a uke.'"

For the October 1998 issue of the music industry trade magazine, *MMR (Musical Merchandise Review)*, I contributed an article headlined, "Is the Ukulele Coming Back?"

Left: Ukulele Masters tour in New York City with (L-R: Led Kaapana, the author, Bob Brozman, Byron Yasui, Lyle Ritz, and Joel Eckhaus). (PHOTO BY ELIZABETH MAIHOCK BELOFF)

Below: Ukulele Masters tour visits the *World News Now* set. (L-R: Paul Syphers, the author, Joel Eckhaus, Bob Brozman, Barry Mitchell, Led Kaapana, Lyle Ritz, and Byron Yasui). (PHOTO BY ELIZABETH MAIHOCK BELOFF)

Hal Leonard had helped set this up, and it allowed me to speak directly to music store owners about why they might want to reconsider their uke offerings. Here's how I opened the article: "Like a comet on some sort of 30–40-year revolution, it seems that the ukulele is once again exerting its gravitational pull on Earth." I then rattled off the evidence, the *Los Angeles Times* article, the sold-out "Legends of Ukulele" concert, the Ukulele Masters tour, supply problems in Hawai'i, and that Roy Sakuma's most recent uke fest jumped from four thousand to six thousand attendees. I also acknowledged another young Hawaiian musician who was inspiring a new generation of players. "Typifying this trend is the band Pure Heart, led by young uke-tyro, Jake Shimabukuro, who can rip a solo on the humble four-stringer that would make Hendrix, Santana and George Harrison (a major uke fan) smile."

Because of the targeted audience, I reviewed the various uke sizes, tunings, portability, kid-friendliness, low-cost entry, as well as the opportunity for repair work on Grandma's old Martin. Also included was a list of almost two dozen companies in Hawai'i and on the mainland that were currently making ukuleles. Finally, I pitched the pleasure of group participation, "Talk to most people about their memories of the ukulele and you'll hear them mention that some family member played one and that they have fond recollections of family singalongs with that uke as the musical center. Lately all of the signs suggest that the pleasure that comes from playing and sharing music with friends and family is something that will be with us for a long time to come."

On one of our trips back East that fall, we visited Dale and Phyllis in their New Hartford, Connecticut, home. While there, Dale made a surprise presentation. In his typically quiet, understated way, Dale had been working on a prototype of a new ukulele unlike any other. Using a toaster oven to cast the fretboard and a kitchen oven for the back-shell, he constructed a nontraditional instrument with molded components that could stand up on its end. The neck and unique open-headstock were made of solid maple and the soundboard was Australian hoop pine. Although it was just a prototype, it sounded good enough for us to consider presenting it at the 1999 NAMM show in late January.

On the flight back to Los Angeles, Liz began to play with possible names for this new instrument. She started thinking about words that included the letters "uke," which eventually led to "Fluke." The word "fluke" was especially promising for several reasons. It conjured up a surprising bit of luck or a happy accident, which rang true for all of us. Fluke could also refer to the triangular end of a boat anchor or a whale's tail, which echoed the triangular soundboard shape. Another bit of synchronicity was that the first two letters of Fluke were also the first two letters of Flea as in Flea Market Music. All agreed that "Fluke" worked, and Liz set about designing a logo.

Liz's Fluke doodle on an American Airlines napkin. (COURTESY OF FLEA MARKET MUSIC, INC.)

After the sold-out "Legends of Ukulele" show at McCabe's Guitar Shop in August, it was clear that there was a significant audience for an all-ukulele evening, and so we booked another concert a few months later. On Sunday, October 25, we put on two shows at 7 and 9:30 p.m., and both of those sold out as well. Special guest artists that night included Lyle Ritz, who happened to be in town, and Bruce Belland, the cowriter of the late 1950s hit song by The Four Preps, "26 Miles (Santa Catalina)." Bruce co-wrote the song on a baritone ukulele and, of course, reprised it that night.

McCabe's Guitar Shop also became the home of an ongoing series of ukulele workshops I taught along with Travis Harrelson and John Zhender. Usually, I would teach a beginner's workshop myself and then follow that with a more advanced work-shop that included Travis and John. These workshops were generally ninety minutes to two hours long and many of the beginners would stay for the advanced class, even if it was beyond their abilities. The turnout for these sessions was large enough that they had to be held in the "concert" room. As word spread, fifty or more attendees per workshop were not uncommon, and because so many were regulars, we got to know them on a first-name basis. A typical beginner workshop would start with instruction on how to hold and tune the uke, making chords and strums, and then playing through some easy songs together. An advanced workshop might include a review of chord inversions, choosing uke-friendly keys to play in, fingerpicking patterns, and playing through more challenging chord solo arrangements.

Everyone brainstorms in different ways. Liz always felt she was more creative if she was actually chewing when she was "chewing on an idea." With so much recent media interest, so many new projects in the pipeline, and the debut of the Fluke for the upcoming NAMM show, we couldn't help but think that the future of the ukulele was looking especially bright. One day while having lunch at a fast-food Asian restaurant in Studio City, Liz blurted out, "Uke Can Change the World." In that moment, Liz condensed our dreams for Flea Market Music and the musical instrument we were promoting into a memorable five-word slogan.

The Pasadena Doo Dah Parade has been an annual tradition in Pasadena, Cali-fornia, since 1978. Dreamed up in a local bar, it was meant to be a finger in the eye of the far more respectable and better known, Pasadena Tournament of Roses, Rose Parade, which also occurred each year in Pasadena. The Doo Dah Parade attracts all

Right: "Uke Can Change the World" logo. (COURTESY OF FLEA MARKET MUSIC, INC.)

Below: The Rhino gang (and the author) dressed like Tiny Tim for the 1998 Doo Dah Parade. (PHOTO BY ELIZABETH MAIHOCK BELOFF)

sorts of conceptually silly and absurd participants like the Lawn Mower or Briefcase Drill Teams and on November 22, Rhino Records employees decided to use the *Legends of Ukulele* CD as their parade theme. In particular, they were going to march wearing black jackets, Hawaiian shirts, and Tiny Tim wigs . . . oh, and strumming ukuleles. It was a wonderfully silly and joyous way to wrap up our first year in our own business. A year that went far beyond our wildest expectations.

George

The repercussions from the 1999 NAMM in late January were also beyond all expectations. Once again, the trade show was held at the Los Angeles Convention Center. This time, though, rather than just attending, Flea Market Music took a booth. Although the costs associated with this—the space, carpeting, electricity, furniture, etcetera—were not insignificant, the response more than justified the investment. The day before the show, Dale flew in from Connecticut to help set up. Several prototype Flukes had been shipped in advance. All were concert length (slightly longer than the most common, soprano size). They also sported three different colored soundboards—yellow, orange, and green.

As it happens, Liz's college friend and Harvard Business School graduate, Cindy Kerr, was visiting as well, and she was able to help Dale crunch some realistic wholesale and retail pricing, and even a special offer for dealers who bought all three colors. We also realized that we needed to come up with more colorful names for those three soundboard hues. Yellow became "Pineapple," orange became "Mango," and green became "Uke-alyptus." Along with an emphasis on the Fluke being entirely manufactured in the United States, here is some copy from an early promotional flyer:

Created to respond to the current surge in popularity of the ukulele worldwide, the FLUKE is aimed at both current players as well as the players of tomorrow. Designed with quality materials chosen for acoustics and durability, this four-stringed instrument offers high value at almost impulse prices. Eye-catchingly colorful, it is easy to play and hard to put down.

For parents who are looking for an inexpensive first instrument for their kids, for current players who want an additional uke to take to the beach, for senior citizens who are looking for a musical outlet, for anyone who wants to discover the joys of making their own music, this FLUKE is very much a stroke of good luck.

These days, NAMM is flooded with booths of ukulele makers, but at the 1999 Winter NAMM, Flea Market Music was the only vendor that specialized entirely in ukuleles and related products. To give the booth some personality, we rented a six-foot potted palm tree and Liz tracked down several feet of green raffia that we wrapped around the counter-height display table to suggest a hula skirt. We even had a rack of plastic leis as giveaways. The booth also included a "players" chair as well as a listening station with headphones where guests could sample my two solo CDs and the Rhino compilation. All of our Jumpin' Jim's songbooks to date were on display, as was the ukulele history book.

Although Dale had yet to commit to the tooling for the back-shell mold, we took close to two hundred Fluke orders at the show. Interest was particularly keen among Japanese wholesalers and dealers who told us that the ukulele was very popular in Japan and that they were having a hard time finding quality instruments to meet the demand. Experienced instrument builders also stopped by to examine the Fluke. They gave Dale positive feedback on his unique design, along with thoughts on improving the sound and simplifying the manufacturing. Once again, we were reminded of the generous spirit that ran through the fretted-instrument maker community.

Throughout the four days, we also received a fair amount of ribbing from pass-ersby who thought we had landed in the wrong decade. Others smiled and twittered "Tiptoe Thru' the Tulips" as they hurried by. However, a healthy number of other attendees were happy to see us and thought that our ukulele dreams were well placed. One of those was Danny Ferrington, a longtime master luthier to the stars. Danny had designed and built guitars for George Harrison, Eric Clapton, Elvis Costello, Johnny Cash, Linda Ronstadt, Jackson Browne, Stephen Bishop, and many others. He also loved ukuleles.

As he was walking by our booth, he recognized the ukulele history book and stopped in. It turned out that Danny had just received the book as a "Christmas gift from George." Liz and I were alone in the booth at that moment and we both asked

The Flea Market Music booth at the 1999 NAMM show. (PHOTO BY ELIZABETH MAIHOCK BELOFF)

The author and Dale Webb at the 1999 NAMM show. (PHOTO COURTESY OF *MUSICAL MERCHANDISE REVIEW*)

Danny who "George" was. Danny said, "You know, George, George Harrison." Wow. Then Danny told us that George was currently in Los Angeles and would like to stop by our house and see our ukulele collection, perhaps next week. Double wow! We gave Danny our contact information and, remarkably, said and thought little about it. We told almost no one. In retrospect, I guess it was because in our hearts, we knew that Beatles don't come to your house.

Several days later, on February 2, we were still doubtful even as Danny kept calling with hourly updates on the stops he and George were making, as they were slowly heading our way. I couldn't help humming George's song, "Blue Jay Way," about waiting at home for friends that never seem to arrive. Then sometime in the early afternoon, Danny Ferrington and George Harrison walked into our living room. My first memory was that George grabbed a banjo uke resting on a stand and began to strum and sing the old George Formby classic, "Leaning on a Lamp-post," which later became a hit for Herman's Hermits. For the next three hours after that, we talked ukuleles and strummed songs. George shared several originals that eventually ended up on his posthumously released *Brainwashed* album. I even summoned the nerve to play him a couple of my songs. He also brought with him a new video camera, which he used to document our vintage uke collection. George was interested in collecting, as well.

Amazingly, at the time of George's visit, Liz and I were at work on *Jumpin' Jim's '60s Uke-In* songbook, which was to include many Beatles songs and two by George. We were especially excited about this book, because it was going to be the first to feature songs we grew up with in the 1960s, and we were surprised and delighted at how good they sounded on the ukulele. I pointed out the Beatles' classic tune, "All My Loving," as an example. A moment later, Liz, Danny, George Harrison, and I were singing and strumming "All My Loving." Liz and I stole a look at each other as if to say, "Freeze this on your retina—it doesn't get better than this."

There are two other moments from that afternoon that are worth sharing: The first came about toward the end of the visit when I asked George if he would be willing to write a short note on why he liked the ukulele. I gave him a piece of Flea Market Music stationery, and he sat at our dining table and composed the charming paragraph with the funny, little drawings that became the "Appreciation" in the *'60s Uke-In* songbook. The other memorable moment happened as George and Danny were leaving. At the

2/2/99.

Everybody should have and play a 'UKE' its so simple to carry with you and it is one instrument you cant play and not laugh! Its so sweet and also very old — some are made of wood — some are made of armadillo's. I love them — the more the merrier — Everyone I know who is into the Ukulele is 'crackers' so get yourself a few and enjoy yourselves — love from George (Keoki) Harrison

Some are made from pigs!

The George Harrison "Appreciation." (COURTESY OF FLEA MARKET MUSIC, INC.)

end of our goodbyes, George ran over to the piano and grandly played the intro to his most famous song, "Something." And with that, he said, "See you later" and dashed off.

As Danny and George drove away, Liz and I stood in stunned silence. We waited about a minute and then we let loose the Beatlemania scream we'd been holding inside for three hours. At that moment, we became convinced that George's visit was a sign that we were following the right path.

UKEtopia

On March 14, 1999, we were back at McCabe's for another installment of our all-uku-lele revue. By now, we had broadened the repertoire for these shows beyond the scope of the Rhino *Legends of Ukulele* compilation, and, thus, a new name was needed. After a brainstorming session with Liz, "UKEtopia" was born, a place we likened to "Ukulele Heaven on Earth." We did, however, keep the basic format of the prior shows, with a dozen or so uke-based solo artists, duos, or groups performing two to three songs each with backup provided by Fred Sokolow on guitar and Jeff Falkner on acoustic bass. Because so many of the artists themselves were experienced musicians, they often backed each other up as well.

There were two new elements we added to this first UKEtopia that became inte-gral parts of the show's future DNA. The first was that I opened the concert with a short original theme song, "UKEtopia." It was meant to cast a spell on everyone in the room:

> There's a place I'd like to take you to,
> The kind of place for folks like me and you,
> You'll feel better once you've been through,
> UKEtopia, UKEtopia.
>
> If your life's a bit too humdrum,
> If your load's a bit cumbersome,
> Won't you stop by for a strum?
> UKEtopia, UKEtopia!

The second was inspired by earlier audience members toting ukuleles. If this was truly UKEtopia, then every uke-toting member of the audience should get to play as well. We decided the best time to have that happen would be at the end of the show. McCabe's could seat 150 in their concert room and many of those attending would have ukes that might or might not be in tune. The solution for that was to tune everyone up just before intermission, which would help build excitement.

The other challenge was how to share the music we were going to play together. At first, we thought we would make photocopies of the chords and lyrics and pass them out as people were seated. But to read the music at the end of the show would require raising the house lights which would break the spell and leave everyone staring at the handouts. Ultimately, Liz came up with an idea that made it even more of an experience. Because the final songs were always well known and involved only a handful of chords, Liz had the chord names and fingering grids blown up and glued to 20 by 30-inch sheets of foam core. Just before we tuned everyone up, she asked for audience volunteers to hold up each chord.

Then, just before the audience strum-along, she had the volunteers line up in front of the stage with their chord blowups. She explained that when they saw her point to them, they should hold their chord high above their heads. As the entire UKEtopia cast performed the closing songs with the audience, Liz conducted her volunteers so the audience could see the correct chord and play along. On March 14, the two closing songs were "Aloha 'Oe" and "Don't Worry, Be Happy." It was magic. The volunteers, who Liz called "chord-a-teers," relished their moment in the limelight, the audience loved strumming and singing with the performers and word spread that UKEtopia shows were loads of fun. Everyone floated out of McCabe's on a UKEtopian cloud. This was a typical response: "Dude, great show at McCabe's last night! That was my second show, and I can't wait for the next."

With the March 14 show, we also established the idea of a permanent cast of players plus a rotating set of special guest artists. Over the years, regulars included Ian and Regina Whitcomb, who always performed in the penultimate spot, Lyle Ritz, Bill Tapia, Janet Klein, Travis Harrelson, Shep "Mr. Ukulele" Stern, John Zhender, Rick Cunha, Denny "King Kukulele" Moynahan, Larry "D" Duplechan, Fred Sokolow, and Jeff Falkner. Liz and I produced the shows, and I emceed. For the March show, our

UKEtopia show finale 3/14/99. (L-R: John Zhender, Chuck Fayne, Travis Harrelson, Shep "Mr. Ukulele" Stern, the author, Bergman Broom, Ian Whitcomb, Janet Klein, Peter Brooke Turner, Fred Sokolow, Denny "King Kukulele" Moynahan, Jeff Falkner, and Rick Cunha). (PHOTO BY ROBERT LESLIE DEAN)

special guests included Chuck "Frets" Fayne, who happened to be in town from Australia, Dan "Cool Hand Uke" Scanlan, and Victoria Jackson from *Saturday Night Live*, who strummed a few original songs including, "A Nice Ukulele."

As was so often the case those days, one thing led to another. After the March show, several of us from UKEtopia became involved with a new film, *Stanley's Gig*, about a troubled uke player who has dreams of being an entertainer on cruise ships. William Sanderson, best known for his work on the *Newhart* TV show and the movie, *Blade Runner*, was cast as Stanley. Faye Dunaway played Stanley's good friend, Leila, and Marla Gibbs played Eleanor Whitney, a retired jazz singer. The only problem was that Sanderson couldn't play the uke or sing. The director and producers all attended UKEtopia and came away eager to tap many of us in one way or another for the film. Ultimately, they had Ian Whitcomb dub the singing and playing for Stanley in the movie. Ian also

113

Stanley's Gig CD. (COURTESY OF RICH DICKERSON, 4JOHNNY RECORDS / ATHER ENTERTAINMENT)

wrote several delightful songs for the film. When the movie was released in June 2000, my song, "For the Love of Uke," had also made it into the film.

At the same time, Liz and I were wrapping up two new songbooks, *'60s Uke-In* and *Gone Hawaiian*, so that they could debut at the Summer NAMM show in Nashville, Tennessee. *Jumpin' Jim's '60s Uke-In* was the first songbook I took a direct role in arranging. Part of the reason was that many of the hit songs of the 1960s were written for guitar, which meant that they were sometimes in keys that were difficult for ukulele players. On top of that, the recordings were often notably sung by males with high tenor voices.

When I began arranging the Beatles songs for the book, it never occurred to me to change the original keys. They were sacrosanct, I thought, and so I just went with the original keys whether they were uke-friendly or not. After the twenty-five songs were arranged, I then played through the book as a future purchaser might. First, I was struck by how many of the songs featured chords that would be difficult for beginners and advanced beginners to play. And then I realized, with some dismay, that many of the songs in the book were pitched too high for me to sing comfortably. I wouldn't even be able to enjoy my own songbook. I was at a crossroads.

I called Hal Leonard, who controlled the print licensing for the Beatles catalog, to see if I could transpose the songs to more uke-friendly keys. Thankfully, the answer was "yes." With that in mind, I developed an approach to arranging that I thought would satisfy a majority of players. Essentially, it was to find the sweet spot between a ukulele-friendly playing key, like C, F, and G and possibly D and A, and a melody that wasn't too high or too low. I knew I was in the ballpark if Liz and I could both sing the song.

For the *'60s Uke-In* front cover, Liz found some "groovy" period typefaces and, of course, added "With an appreciation by George Harrison." Our uke-pun affliction contributed the "It's Ukedelic!" copy line on the back cover where my floating head ended up in the center of a flower. Ten of the twenty-five "fab" songs were from the Beatles' catalog with the rest coming from the Beach Boys,

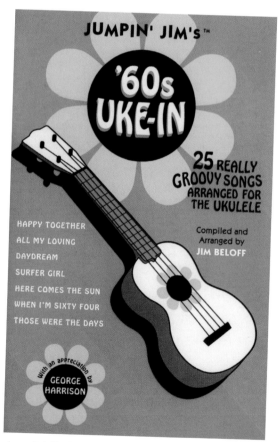

Jumpin' Jim's '60s Uke-In cover. (COURTESY OF FLEA MARKET MUSIC, INC.)

Monkees, Otis Redding, Donovan, The Turtles, and others. And, yes, we included the Lovin' Spoonful's "Daydream" by John Sebastian. We also filled any empty space with photographs. Going through some old family albums, I found a picture of me in the early 1960s wearing a Beatles sweatshirt. That ended up in the foreword, where I wrote about how good these pop songs sounded on the uke and the "dream come true" of spending an afternoon with George Harrison. We also found a good use for a photo Liz took of me with the Beatles at Madame Tussauds Wax Museum in London.

Since many of the thirty classic Hawaiian tunes in *Gone Hawaiian* were written by a handful of songwriters, we added short biographical sketches of Sonny Cunha, "My Honolulu Hula Girl"; Johnny Noble, "My Little Grass Shack in Kealakekua, Hawaii"; R. Alex Anderson, "Lovely Hula Hands"; Don McDiarmid, "Little Brown Gal"; Harry Owens, "Sweet Leilani"; Jack Owens, "The Hukilau Song"; and Leon Pober, who wrote "Tiny Bubbles," the Don Ho hit.

Songs of a certain age, including many from the Tin Pan Alley era, had introductory verses. Typically, the verse was meant to set up the chorus or the main part of the song. Due to space limitations, and because most people didn't know these less-performed verses, we would usually omit them from our songbooks. There were exceptions, however. One in particular was the delightful intro to "Ukulele Lady." Another was the intro to "Waikiki" by Andy Cummings, one of the most beautiful songs in *Gone Hawaiian*. The book had already been carefully laid out and engraved when I first heard the introductory verse to "Waikiki." It was equally beautiful and, I thought, essential. I talked to Charylu to see if we could squeeze the additional measures onto the two pages we had already allotted for the song, but there seemed to be no possible way. We looked hard at the "roadmap," which was what we called the space-saving format that involved putting repeated sections under each other, but there still wasn't enough room for the additional twelve measures. That night I decided to share our struggle with the spirit of Andy Cummings. I sent a prayer out to him with the hope that he could help me figure out how to reformat the song in such a way that we could get his entire song, verse, and chorus, onto the two pages. When I woke up the next morning, I had a new roadmap possibility, and it worked.

Jumpin' Jim's Gone Hawaiian cover. (COURTESY OF FLEA MARKET MUSIC, INC.)

The media continued to beat the drum about the third wave of uke popularity. In the January issue of *Acoustic Guitar*, resident uke expert, Michael Simmons wrote a combined review of *The Joy of Uke* video, and the *For the Love of Uke* and *Legends of Ukulele* CDs, titled, "The Joy of Uke." Subtitled: "Jim Beloff Leads the 20th Century's Third Ukulele Revival," Simmons reviewed the prior two waves, and wrote: "As the millennium closes, the ukulele is undergoing its third surge in popularity this century." Joe Hagan in the February/March issue of *Civilization* magazine wrote his own story titled, "Uke Can Take It with You," which quoted Stan Werbin, owner of Elderly Instruments in Lansing, Michigan: "We're selling twice as many as ten years ago . . . we're calling it the instrument of the twenty-first century."

The third "surge" was also leading to new ukulele festivals on the Mainland. In April, we drove to Hayward, California, for the 'Ukulele Festival of Northern California. This one-day festival was begun in 1994, "To promote and perpetuate the playing of 'ukulele music and culture by bringing all ages and levels together to share 'ukulele talent." Seven hundred uke fans attended that year, and Liz and I sold a lot of books, videos, and CDs and took orders for the Fluke. I also performed as part of the all-day line-up of players.

The author and Liz in the Flea Market Music booth at the "Ukulele festival of Northern California." (AUTHOR'S COLLECTION)

Peter and Donna Thomas with one of their books made out of an actual ukulele.
(PHOTO BY ELIZABETH MAIHOCK BELOFF)

The day before Hayward, we were invited to a "Ukulele Extravaganza" at the home of Peter and Donna Thomas in Santa Cruz. Peter and Donna were "book" artists who had created a series of books made out of actual ukuleles. That day, a group of their musician friends, along with Liz, me, and Janet Klein from Los Angeles gathered to socialize, play ukes, and entertain each other. Local guests included Oliver Brown, Mark Kapner, Pat "Tiki King" Baron, Rick "Ukulele Dick" McKee, uke luthier Tony Graziano, and uke collector Sandor Nagyszalanczy. Peter along with Andy Andrews would eventually go on to found the Santa Cruz Ukulele Club in 2002, one of the first and largest ukulele clubs in the country.

Japan

At Roy Sakuma's ukulele festival, we met many players from Japan, and over time became friends with Masami "Matt" Kobayashi who was a member of NUA, the Nihon Ukulele Association, founded in 1959. After the release of the history book and the Rhino CD, Matt invited Liz and me to Japan for the fortieth-anniversary celebration of NUA in early June 1999.

The author with Machiko and Masami "Matt" Kobayashi. (PHOTO BY ELIZABETH MAIHOCK BELOFF)

The trip to Japan was another example of how much our lives were changed thanks to the ukulele. In preparation for the trip, Liz took a class in conversational Japanese at a nearby school and then shared the basics with me. In the meantime, Matt and other NUA members made arrangements for our week there, building in time for us to tour Kamakura and Kobe as well as meet with top Japanese uke players, retailers, and manufacturers. The trip was extraordinary in every way. For the formal event, I gave a lecture on the great players of the ukulele, adapted from the Rhino CD liner notes. The presentation was given in a ceremonial room on the top floor of Yamano Gakki, a leading music store in the Ginza shopping district of Tokyo. I spoke to a group of seventy guests in English and then paused while it was translated into Japanese. After discussing each player, a short sample of their track was played from the Rhino compilation.

After the presentation, Liz and I were escorted to a nearby beer restaurant where there were two hundred partygoers, both members of NUA and guests, already in a celebratory mood. The room included a stage and Liz and I performed, along with many of the NUA members. I'd been requested to sing "Big in Japan," an original song from the *For the Love of Uke* CD. The first verse was:

Can't get arrested here,
But I'm big in Japan.
Go unmolested here,
But I'm big in Japan.
The girls they meet my plane,
Mob me on the bullet train.
I'm unknown in Bangor, Maine,
But I'm big in Japan.

Everybody sang along. And then we sang one classic Tin Pan Alley or Hawaiian song after another. The NUA members knew them all. The beer, no doubt, was a lubricant, but the goodwill that we felt from everyone that day was genuine.

The next morning, Matt took us on the Shinkansen bullet train from Tokyo to Kobe. Juji Iwamoto, also a member of NUA, had invited us to come to Kobe to sightsee and attend a dinner with the Kobe Hawaiian Club. For Liz and me it was another "pinch me" moment where you can't quite believe that you're sitting in a beautiful restaurant in the mountains overlooking Kobe, Japan, eating Kobe beef while people around you are playing ukuleles. The tour of the city was also memorable. Kobe had experienced a major earthquake on January 17, 1995, exactly one year after the Northridge earthquake Liz and I had experienced. Although the loss of life and damage in Kobe was magnitudes greater, four years later, the city had bounced back.

Before returning to Tokyo, we toured a bit of Osaka and then were treated to the finest sushi meal I've ever had. Our host was Isami Uchizaki, a college professor, who we'd met a few days earlier at the Yamano Gakki ceremony, where he spoke about the history of the ukulele. Uchizaki-san had a world-class vintage uke collection and we shared stories about our rarest finds.

Another high point of the trip was spending time with Kazuyuki Sekiguchi, best known as the bass guitar player for the hugely successful Japanese pop music group,

the Southern All Stars. Sekiguchi-san was also known for his deep interest in the ukulele, which began after seeing Mia Farrow playing one in *The Purple Rose of Cairo*. We
met him at Nofofon Bears, a store that he and his wife owned in Tokyo that specialized in stuffed bears and ukuleles. At Nofofon, we also met Kenji Kawai who taught
ukulele at the store. Kenji had studied in the United States for a while, and his English
was excellent. When we met Kenji, he had already translated much of my ukulele history book and was hoping it might lead to a Japanese edition. While in Tokyo, we also
met with some prominent musical instrument dealers and distributors who were very
interested in the Fluke. By the time we left Japan, we had accumulated several large
orders and many individual sales, which we happily passed along to Dale and Phyllis.

Left: The author at the 40th anniversary celebration of the Nihon
Ukulele Association in Tokyo in
1999. (PHOTO BY ELIZABETH MAIHOCK
BELOFF)

Below: NUA 40th anniversary
party at a Tokyo beer restaurant.
(PHOTO BY ELIZABETH MAIHOCK BELOFF)

Above: Kenji Kawai, the author, and Sekiguchi-san at Nofofon Bears in Tokyo. (PHOTO BY ELIZABETH MAIHOCK BELOFF)

Left: Member of the Kobe Hawaiian Club playing a Fluke. (PHOTO BY ELIZABETH MAIHOCK BELOFF)

Uke Can't Be Serious

Once we were home from Japan, my most pressing task was to find someone to orchestrate the ukulele concerto. Ever since Phil Ventre had commissioned the piece the year before, I had been developing the ukulele part. Fortunately, before our conversation, I had banked a few instrumental themes that I thought might work as motifs for a larger piece of music. The bigger question was whether I should acknowledge in some musical way that this concerto was a first of its kind. Should I draw attention to that fact, or ignore it and present a new work that just happened to feature a solo ukulele?

In the end, I did both. The opening and closing sections of the ten-minute concerto would sound perfectly at home in a classical music setting. The middle was something else entirely. My idea was that after establishing in the first five minutes that the instrument could, in fact, share the stage with a symphony orchestra, it would revert to its better-known personality—as an accompaniment to a song. In this case, I wrote "Uke Can't Be Serious," a jazzy, humorous tune that addressed head-on the foolhardy notion of a ukulele in an orchestral setting. This was the lyric:

> Uke can't be serious,
> It's not your way,
> Uke can't be serious,
> At night or day,
> At times delirious,
> You never weary us, it's true,
> And now we're serious for you.

> Uke can't be classical,
> It's not your thing,
> You're such a rascal,
> A summer fling.
> Refined and dignified,
> The very model of restraint,
> These are all the things you ain't.

124

We expect Rachmaninoff
You would turn him on and off . . .

We expect Sibelius,
You, you ukulele us . . .

Uke can't be serious,
It's not your style,
Try to be serious,
You make us smile.
So insignificant,
And yet . . . if we can't have you,
We'd be so seriously blue,
You see we're serious,
I know it's quite mysterious,
But we're so serious for you!

While I heard more thoughtful and stirring orchestrations for the front and back sections, I wanted a jazzy "pops" orchestra sound for the interior song. Then, as the song finishes, the soloist (me) suddenly realizes where he is (a classical music concert) and steers his ukulele back to the opening classical motifs for the big finale.

Thanks to a recommendation from a composer friend, Jason Nyberg entered the scene with about four months to orchestrate the concerto, now titled, *Uke Can't Be Serious*. Fortunately, Jason was the perfect choice. Not only was he able to work quickly, but Jason really understood the contrasting moods that were necessary to make it work. As a result, he brought surprising depth to the "classical" sections and a swingy light touch to the center song. The finale was exciting and triumphant. Jason finished the score in time for Phil to rehearse it for the November premiere. The venue would be the Paul Mellon Arts Center at Choate, my old playground.

Phil had also asked me to have an encore prepared. It occurred to me that my song, "Charles Ives," would be appropriate and I forwarded Rick Cunha's arrangement from the *For the Love of Uke* CD.

While the concerto was coming together, Liz and I were busy keeping many other plates spinning. We attended the Summer NAMM in Nashville with Phyllis and Dale, where we continued the rollout of the Fluke, now with a new "Plum" color and amplification options. We also put on another UKEtopia at McCabe's with special guests Rick "Ukulele Dick" McKee from Santa Cruz and Andy Powers from Carlsbad, a remarkable seventeen-year-old musician who was building his own line of high-end ukuleles. Andy would eventually go on to become the master guitar designer and partner at Taylor Guitars.

A lot of time and attention was also going into upgrading our website so that it could process online orders. By 1999, all of our products were available online, as well as the Fluke and various accessories. At the time, because few people knew what the Fluke sounded like, I recorded a promotional CD with five original songs, all played on a Fluke. We also added CDs from other artists like Lyle Ritz, Ian Whitcomb, and Janet Klein. We even stocked ukulele-themed Hawaiian shirts. The website also became the home of the "Collector's Uke Yak," a page where people could post questions about vintage ukuleles and their upkeep. Chuck Fayne volunteered to be the "resident expert," and he quickly established the page as a place to get useful information and plenty of laughs.

Having collected thousands of names and addresses of uke enthusiasts in the United States and around the world, we started to send out promotional mailings about our products. At first, it was just one sheet of paper, but that soon evolved into a twice-yearly, sixteen-page catalog we called "MDHF," a bit of insider-ism, which stood for "My Dog Has Fleas." The subtitle was "All Things Ukulele from Flea Market Music" and we had a scratching dog mascot drawn by illustrator, journalist, blogger, and uke fan Mark Frauenfelder. I was responsible for the catalog copy and Liz made it all look good.

We were also navigating invitations for me to give uke workshops, often followed by short performances at music stores, including several in the Northwest. Three, in particular, became regular stops: Gryphon Stringed Instruments in Palo Alto, California, Artichoke Music in Portland, Oregon, and Dusty Strings in Seattle, Washington.

In November, I flew back for the premiere of *Uke Can't Be Serious*. It was to be part of a program celebrating the Wallingford Symphony Orchestra's twenty-fifth anniversary, which included works by Brahms, Copland, Beethoven, and Mahler. Amanda Savio of the local *Record-Journal* newspaper had this to say about the performance:

The 1999 premiere of *Uke Can't Be Serious*, with the Wallingford Symphony Orchestra, Phil Ventre conductor. (The author is center right.) (PHOTO BY ELIZABETH MAIHOCK BELOFF)

The author with conductor Phil Ventre. (PHOTO BY ELIZABETH MAIHOCK BELOFF)

Laughter rarely comes from an audience listening to musicians tune their instruments before playing. However, giggles were heard when Jim Beloff plucked at the strings of his ukulele before launching into the first-ever concerto for ukulele and symphony orchestra, *Uke Can't Be Serious*. The uke was a lovely accompaniment to the fine orchestra, and Beloff provided a sprightly and youthful slant to the music. Some portions of the piece were quite emotional, in fact, and the only downside was that the uke was drowned out by the orchestra in places. At the center of *Uke Can't Be Serious* was a comical song sung by Beloff, which address the lighthearted side of his favorite instrument. Beloff might want to look further into this unusual idea of mixing up the uke with an orchestra—he received shouts of "bravo" and a standing ovation after he finished.

Chapter 4

All Things Ukulele

Firsts

At the start of the new millennium, Flea Market Music, to our pleasant surprise, was becoming a self-supporting enterprise. When people asked us what we did, I got a kick out of saying we were in the "ukulele business," another rarely heard two-word combination. Even so, because Los Angeles was such an entrepreneurial town, the default response was often, "cool." In Connecticut, however, when my mother, Gladys "Mike" Beloff, would update friends about what we were doing, they would voice concern and say (or think), "I'm so sorry."

Nevertheless, we were managing to pay the bills. A colleague of ours who also published music books, got it right when he said that our business was made up of "little oil wells." Between book and CD sales, royalties, workshop gigs, performances, uke fests, and online orders, we had just enough income to get us through the present and underwrite a bit of the future. And so, we pressed on with new songbooks. Thanks to Ronny, we had learned how to write a proposal, license in-copyright songs, do layouts, and road-map arrangements. Just as importantly, we were finding new ways to make our songbooks distinctive, to give them personality.

A good example of that was our next collection, *Jumpin' Jim's Camp Ukulele*, which included forty sing-along songs like "Home on the Range," "Puff, the Magic Dragon," "This Land Is Your Land," and, yes, "Hello Mudduh, Hello Fadduh." For *Camp Ukulele*, we started a new tradition of having a "song audition" night, where we would invite a group of musical friends over to hear and rate a list of possible songs for inclusion. *Camp Ukulele* was a project near and dear to Liz and her cover design featured a constellation of stars shaped like a ukulele on a night sky background. She also placed

Jumpin' Jim's Camp Ukulele cover. (COURTESY OF FLEA MARKET MUSIC, INC.)

Audition night (L-R: Ronny Schiff, Peter Wingerd, Peter Thomas, the author, Larry Dilg, Gene Sculatti, and Mimi Kennedy). (PHOTO BY ELIZABETH MAIHOCK BELOFF)

summer camp photos of family and friends and vintage vacation postcards on the inside covers and internal pages. I contributed a theme song of sorts titled, "Camp Ukulele."

We continued to find ways to add value to our other *Jumpin' Jim's* octavo-sized books. After George Harrison graced the *Jumpin' Jim's '60s Uke-In* book with his appreciation, we approached other well-known uke fans for similar contributions. For *Ukulele Beach Party*, surf-guitar legend Dick Dale wrote how, as a young boy, he would sleep with electrician's tape holding his fingers in place so he could make ukulele chords while playing left-handed. He closed by saying, "If it wasn't for the uke . . . I wouldn't be Dick Dale." Film critic and historian Leonard Maltin wrote the appreciation for *Jumpin' Jim's Gone Hollywood* with a focus on ukuleles and the movies. He also helped me put together a list of uke-featured films, like *Honolulu*, *A Thousand Clowns* and *Joe Versus the Volcano*.

Jumpin' Jim's Ukulele Beach Party cover. (COURTESY OF FLEA MARKET MUSIC, INC.)

Jumpin' Jim's Gone Hollywood cover. (COURTESY OF FLEA MARKET MUSIC, INC.)

Jumpin' Jim's Ukulele Spirit was published after the 9/11 attacks. The book was our response to a new desire to sing songs of peace and faith together. Even before 9/11, we were hearing about gospel music and hymns being *strummed* in churches. For the *Ukulele Spirit* appreciation, we approached Pat Boone, who wrote about the loss of his first Martin baritone on a high school trip to Washington, D.C. Pat also credited the ukulele for easing him into performing and, ultimately, his entertainment career.

Jumpin' Jim's Ukulele Spirit cover. (COURTESY OF FLEA MARKET MUSIC, INC.)

There was another motivating factor that drove the rest of our songbook releases. That was a desire to be *first*. We were first out of the gate to publish a jazz ukulele songbook, followed by other firsts; classical, blues, bluegrass, baroque, and country music. Each one was a new opportunity to widen the perception of what could and should be played on a ukulele.

I also began inviting other virtuosos to arrange books for us. The first to take on the challenge was Lyle Ritz. With his book, *Lyle Ritz: Jazz*, we broke out of our octavo-sized mold and jumped up to a 9 by 12-inch format. It also became the first book in a series we called "Ukulele Masters" that featured arrangements by the very finest players. Each book included a CD or audio download of the arranger performing the pieces. Lyle eventually arranged three books for us in the series. Herb Ohta also arranged a *Ukulele Masters* book of standards that showcased his unique style. I included an interview with Herb that revealed a lot about his technique and his focus on melody as the most important thing in music.

We broke new ground in 2004 with the publication of *The Classical Ukulele* arranged by John King. At the time, John was unquestionably the finest

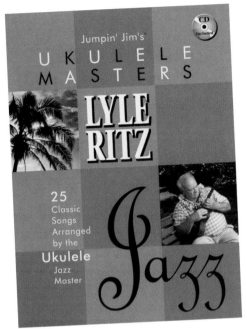

Ukulele Masters: Lyle Ritz Jazz cover. (COURTESY OF FLEA MARKET MUSIC, INC.)

Ukulele Masters: Herb Ohta Sophisticated Ukulele cover. (COURTESY OF FLEA MARKET MUSIC, INC.)

classical ukulele player in the world. He had a background in classical guitar, but his performances of Bach on the ukulele were truly jaw-dropping. As it happened, John was also the preeminent scholar on the history of the instrument and his research revealed that there were historical precedents for performing classical music on the ukulele, going back to its Madeiran roots. *The Classical Ukulele* was our first book to offer the arrangements in both traditional music notation as well as ukulele tablature. Tablature is an entirely different way of reading music, based

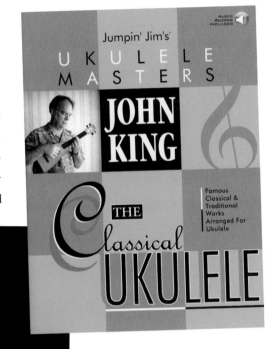

Above: *Ukulele Masters: John King The Classical Ukulele* cover. (COURTESY OF FLEA MARKET MUSIC, INC.)

Left: John King. (PHOTO BY ELIZABETH MAIHOCK BELOFF)

on four lines that represent the strings of the uke and numbers that represent the fret to be played. You didn't need to read music at all to follow the tablature. We had no idea how well the book would be received when it was published, but sixteen years later, it is an evergreen and credited by many with launching the surprisingly passionate, *classical* ukulele community.

In 2011, I received an email from Tony Mizen in England who had arranged some early lute music for the ukulele and wondered if we'd be interested in publishing a book of these arrangements. Our first thought was that we'd sell about four copies. Then we heard recordings of the arrangements and decided it didn't matter how many copies we sold, this needed to be published. Eventually we put out three books of classical music arranged by Tony, in both musical notation and uke tablature. The first, *From Lute to Uke*, included twenty-four pieces, many composed by John Dowland. *The Baroque Ukulele* featured twenty-two works by Bach, Vivaldi, Pachelbel, and other baroque-era composers. And *The Romantic Ukulele* included twenty-two pieces by, among others, Chopin, Debussy, and Satie. All are steady sellers.

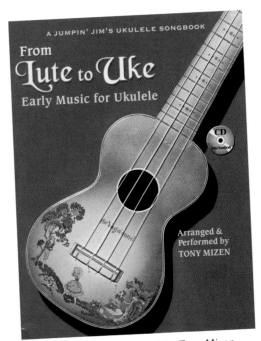

From Lute to Uke Arranged by Tony Mizen cover. (COURTESY OF FLEA MARKET MUSIC, INC.)

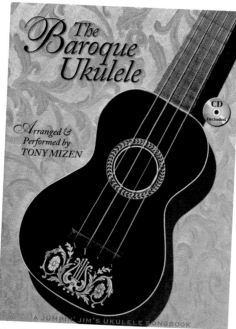

The Baroque Ukulele Arranged by Tony Mizen cover. (COURTESY OF FLEA MARKET MUSIC, INC.)

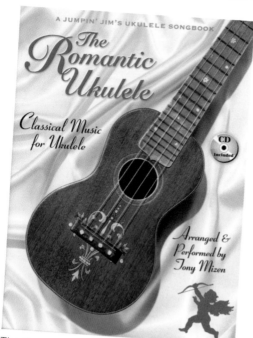

The Romantic Ukulele Arranged by Tony Mizen cover. (COURTESY OF FLEA MARKET MUSIC, INC.)

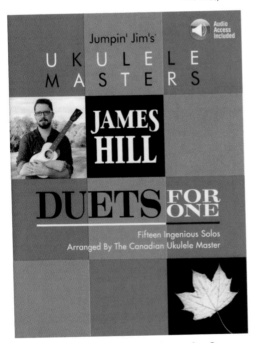

Ukulele Masters: James Hill Duets for One cover. (COURTESY OF FLEA MARKET MUSIC, INC.)

It's worth pointing out that arranging classical music for the ukulele is all about making hard choices. For example, an orchestra can play an unlimited number of notes at one time. A uke player has a maximum of four they can use. When arranging a piece by Bach or Debussy for the ukulele, the arranger is tasked with determining what can be sacrificed or "reduced" from the original music that will still allow the melody and harmony to be present in a satisfying way. The fact that the pieces remain as rich as they are is both a testament to the music itself, as well as the craft of the arranger. The same can also be said for jazz arrangements on the uke. A jazz pianist has ten fingers for ten possible notes to spell out complex chords. The uke player still has only four. The human ear, however, is a sophisticated organ and can "hear" many of the missing notes.

Our sixth *Ukulele Masters* book, *Duets for One*, was published in 2017 and arranged by Canadian uke virtuoso and educator James Hill. There were only a few next-generation players whom we thought were at the same level of Lyle, Herb, and John King, and James was one of them. In *Duets for One*, James arranged old and new popular songs, including Coldplay's "Viva la Vida," in such a way that there was the illusion of two independent parts playing on a single ukulele, once again pushing the boundaries of what could be accomplished on four strings.

Fred Sokolow was part of our musical circle in Los Angeles as both a longtime member of Ian Whitcomb's Bungalow Boys and our UKEtopia cast. In addition to being an ace musician and solo performer on anything with frets, Fred was a prolific method book writer with dozens of titles through Hal Leonard and other publishers. He also arranged three uke books for Flea Market Music. The first two were collections of blues and bluegrass tunes.

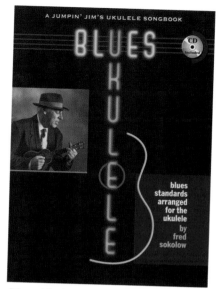

Blues Ukulele by Fred Sokolow cover.
(COURTESY OF FLEA MARKET MUSIC, INC.)

The third, *Jazzing Up the Uke*, was designed to help players take simple arrangements of songs and add harmonic interest to them through the use of chord substitutions. Fred and I also collaborated on a uke edition of his popular *Fretboard Roadmaps* series.

Bluegrass Ukulele by Fred Sokolow cover.
(COURTESY OF FLEA MARKET MUSIC, INC.)

Jazzing Up the Ukulele by Fred Sokolow cover. (COURTESY OF FLEA MARKET MUSIC, INC.)

It was Lyle's second book for us, *Lyle Ritz: Solos*, that led to an opportunity that was too good to pass up. Having read a lot about song catalogs during my years at *Billboard*, I had learned that they rarely came up for sale and, if they did, they were prohibitively expensive. For Lyle's chord solos book, we decided that he should include "Ritz Cracker," an original tune from his first Verve album. This required that I contact the publisher so we could obtain the print license. Lyle told me that the original publisher was Longridge Music, owned by Perry Botkin Sr., best known as Bing Crosby's guitarist. At the time of his Verve albums, Lyle was good friends with Perry's son, songwriter, arranger, and record producer Perry Botkin Jr., who suggested Longridge as a home for Lyle's original songs. This was in the late 1950s, and by 2002 when I was looking to license "Ritz Cracker," the catalog had been sold several times.

Eventually I tracked down the current owners who were happy to license the song, but also shared with me that they were looking to sell the catalog. Perry Sr. had created Longridge Music as a publishing home for many of his L.A.-based musician/ composer friends and among the two hundred or so works were TV series theme songs and cues, jingles, Hawaiian exotica tunes, bachelor pad music, two uke-themed songs by Perry Sr., "Ukey-Ukulele" and "Duke of the Uke," and Lyle's four original songs from his two Verve recordings. Some of the better-known pieces in the catalog included the theme to the *Jim Bowie* TV show; the Ipana toothpaste, "brusha-brusha"; and Ajax cleanser, "Stronger Than Dirt," jingles; "Two Shillelagh O'Sullivan," a song cowritten by Perry Sr. that was recorded by Bing Crosby, and the music Perry Sr. composed for the film noir, *Murder by Contract*. Another song, "Wine, Women and Gold," was written by Eden Ahbez, the famed songwriter of "Nature Boy." The catalog also included Mel Henke's swingin' instrumentals with sound effects and voiceovers that were custom-made for a retro bachelor pad lifestyle.

Because none of these works were earning very much at the time, the cost for the catalog was reasonable, and not long after, Liz and I owned an oddball mix of 1950s-era songs and TV music. Within six months, we'd earned back our investment. *Saturday Night Live* had used "Two Shillelagh O'Sullivan" in a sketch years earlier, and when they renewed the license, the income on that plus some other Longridge earnings put us in the black. Today, royalties on the musical cues from *Jim Bowie*, *The Beverly Hillbillies*, and *The Life and Legend of Wyatt Earp* continue to roll in from reruns playing all over the world. We call them "pennies from heaven." We also were able to exploit some of the songs, like "Duke of the Uke," for our songbooks. Several years later we released, *Paradise Lost & Found*, a CD that included new recordings of many of the exotica songs from the catalog. They were arranged and performed by WAITIKI, a group of talented Boston-based musicians who were able to re-create the sounds of the original (famed bandleader) Arthur Lyman recordings from the 1950s and 1960s.

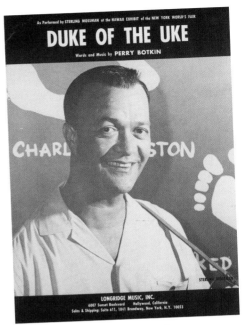

"Duke of the Uke" sheet music.
(COURTESY OF FLEA MARKET MUSIC, INC.)

"Jim Bowie" sheet music. (COURTESY OF FLEA MARKET MUSIC, INC.)

Paradise Lost & Found CD. (COURTESY OF FLEA MARKET MUSIC, INC.)

The desire to be first also translated to other formats and venues. On September 16, 2000, Lyle and Herb Ohta headlined a pair of ukulele jazz concerts I produced at McCabe's. Accompanied by acoustic bassist, Richard Simon, Lyle, and Herb each took a set and then traded licks for the final three songs. The program included jazz standards like "Triste," "Bluesette," "Stompin' at the Savoy," and "Joy Spring." Lyle's daughter, Emily, joined him on an instrumental version of "Tonight You Belong to Me." Harvey Barkan, a reviewer for the local jazz newspaper, *L.A. Jazz Scene*, attended a dry-run concert at Geri's World Coffee House the night before and wrote: "It initially seemed easier to really appreciate the music being produced if I looked away from the ukes periodically and just listened for a while. What a pleasant surprise for my ears; my eyes were slower to put it all together and accept it."

In honor of the concerts, I wrote a new song, "Rare Air." It was a jazzy tune based on an expression that Liz and I used a lot. Whenever we were in the midst of an especially moving experience, music or otherwise, we would whisper to each other, "rare air." At the end of the McCabe's shows, I had the "rare" pleasure of performing the song with both Lyle and Herb as an encore. We recorded the McCabe's performances and put out a CD titled *A Night of Ukulele Jazz: Live at McCabe's* on our Flea Market Music label. It was the first live ukulele jazz recording ever released and, at the time, only the third ukulele jazz recording ever, after Lyle's two Verve albums from the 1950s.

We entered another new world in 2002 when we consulted on "Ukulele Fever," the first museum exhibit on the history of the instrument at the Stamford Museum & Nature Center in Stamford, Connecticut. Sharon Blume, the museum's executive director, had a deep affection for popular culture and after reading my uke history book thought that it would translate well as an exhibit. Liz and I were hired as consultants and we worked very closely with curator, Rosa Portell, to organize the show and gather the most historic and colorful ukes and ephemera. By the February 2, opening day, we had drawn from many private collections to showcase more than a hundred vintage instruments, everything from the rarest Hawaiian and mainland models to the 1950s and 1960s plastic ukes. The exhibit also included period sheet music, advertisements, film clips, movie stills, travel brochures, and ship menus. Around the time of the show, Sharon Blume said, "It's a funny little instrument that caught on as a fad, rather than as a musical endeavor, so it is quite different from any other instrument in the way it

Left: *A Night of Uku-lele Jazz—Live at McCabes* CD. (COURTESY OF FLEA MARKET MUSIC, INC.)

Below: Herb Ohta and Lyle Ritz in the entrance of McCabe's Guitar Shop. (PHOTO BY ELIZABETH MAIHOCK BELOFF)

has been viewed. It was, and is, seen as a playful thing by many, but it can be a serious instrument at the same time."

Besides loaning many of our rarest ukes and ephemera, I made a short film that promised to teach anyone how to play the ukulele in one minute. Alongside the video were Fluke ukes that you could pick up and play along. The opening night celebration featured a variety of performers including Liz and me, Miss Ewa's Hawaiian Trio, and the Battinelli Family Ukesters featuring Pete Zaccagnino. The ukulele was still a hard to resist news story and "Ukulele Fever" generated a small tsunami of local and national press coverage. This culminated with an April 28 segment on CBS *Sunday Morning with Charles Osgood* where he reported from "the great tropical state of Connecticut," presented highlights from the exhibit and strummed with me on "He's Got the Whole World in His Hands."

Ukulele Fever opening display panel. (PHOTO BY HARRY LEVENSTEIN)

Ukulele Fever plastics display panel. (PHOTO BY HARRY LEVENSTEIN)

Ukulele Fever panel. (PHOTO BY HARRY LEVENSTEIN)

The author with Rosa Portell at the Ukulele Fever exhibit in Stamford, Connecticut.
(PHOTO BY ELIZABETH MAIHOCK BELOFF)

The author, Charles Osgood, and Liz at the Ukulele Fever exhibit. (AUTHOR'S COLLECTION)

The Daily Ukulele

Liz and I moved from Los Angeles to Connecticut in 2004. The move was precipitated by a need to be closer to Liz's parents, who were becoming increasingly fragile. Another prod came from a uke fest we attended in San Diego that year. As usual, we had taken a booth and brought a lot of product to sell. After setting up, I walked around the site to see who else was exhibiting and discovered a local music store had taken a booth. Not only that, but they had brought a variety of our books to sell. This was unusual. In those days, most vendors at these fests were part-time sellers of Hawaiian goods and T-shirts, solo instrument builders, strap crafters, artists with their CDs and merch, and small companies like us who focused exclusively on uke products. My first thought was that they were encroaching on our turf. After taking a breath, it dawned on me that this was exactly what we had been working so hard to accomplish. Finally, the ukulele was profitable enough that music stores were willing to set up shop at a weekend uke fest. And, thankfully, they were selling our products. At least on the West Coast, we thought, "our work here is done."

We also realized that our business could be run from anywhere. As soon as we settled down on the Connecticut shoreline, we picked up where we left off and new books and CDs began to roll off the proverbial assembly line. The germ of what became our most ambitious songbook project also began to take root.

One of the major subgroups within the ukulele third wave was semiretired and retired players. Many had been playing before the current wave, but most were new to the instrument and eager to pick it up as a way to stay active and keep learning. There was mounting evidence that playing a musical instrument enhanced brain function, increased memory skills, and made you happier. The ukulele was also, uniquely, a social instrument. Players naturally liked to strum and sing with other players. A phenomenon of this was that a group of a hundred players, all with different abilities, all slightly out of tune with one another, still sounded good when strumming together.

It wasn't long before groups started to meet regularly to play and sing and socialize. One of the very first clubs, formed well before the third wave, was the Oasis Ukulele Strummers who met at the Oasis Senior Center in Newport Beach, California. Led by "master at arms" Tony Cappa, the group would meet every Monday morning to strum through vintage oldies and Hawaiian classics. Along with their ukes, everyone brought their big three-ring notebook of hundreds of photocopied songs specially arranged for the club. Another group, The Ukulele Club of Santa Cruz, begun in 2002, attracted a younger demographic, and they had their own large books filled with more contemporary songs. As these clubs began to proliferate around the country and internationally, there seemed to be a need for a standard book filled with hundreds of well-known, multigenerational songs with easy arrangements, specially created for groups.

With this specific audience in mind, we developed *The Daily Ukulele*. Given the title, our challenge was to compile and arrange 365 well-known songs that would sound especially good played and sung in groups. One of the earliest considerations regarding a book of this size was the binding. We knew that to be successful, the book would have to fold flat. Thanks to the Hal Leonard production team, we found our solution with a comb binding. Another big consideration for Flea Market Music was the cost involved in printing such a large book and the time involved in licensing hundreds of songs. Although many songs were controlled by Hal Leonard, and a good many were public domain classics, there were still plenty that were controlled by other publishing companies. They would need to be researched, contacted, and sent licenses, all of which can be a lengthy process. Ultimately, we realized that we couldn't publish this book alone. Fortunately, Hal Leonard agreed to partner with us to make the book a reality. By doing so, we not only shared the profits, but we also shared the significant costs. And, Hal Leonard offered to clear all the songs and take responsibility for paying the royalties. That was a huge relief.

Liz came up with the subtitle, *365 Songs for Better Living*, after admiring a vintage booklet on maintaining a healthy diet. We used the theme of music as part of a healthy lifestyle in the book's foreword:

> Along with an apple a day, a daily allowance of vitamins and minerals and a daily constitutional . . . playing music regularly is one of the healthiest lifestyle habits you can practice. . . . For those of you who have played a musical instrument, or total beginners who have always longed to play, this book, along with a ukulele, is your key to musical health and happiness. In *The Daily Ukulele*, you'll find easy arrangements of hundreds of great, time-tested tunes at your fingertips.

. . . One thing we've learned in all of our years of publishing ukulele songbooks is that the uke is a very social musical instrument. This would explain
the recent growth of ukulele clubs throughout the United States and the rest
of the world.

. . . Over the years we've seen many worn copies of our other Jumpin'
Jim's songbooks. We take special pride in seeing these especially "loved" cop-
ies, because they have clearly been enjoyed. Here's hoping that this copy of
The Daily Ukulele will become just as "loved."

Like our other songbooks, we took advantage of any empty space on a page. In
particular, we placed vintage photos of people playing ukes that we'd collected over the
years from flea markets, paper shows, and eBay. Although virtually none of the photos had any identifying information, Liz couldn't help wondering if someday someone
would contact us and say that the photo on page such and such was their dad or mom
or another family member. That has actually happened four times since then.

The Daily Ukulele cover.
(COURTESY OF FLEA MARKET
MUSIC, INC./HAL LEONARD LLC)

149

Right: Well-loved *Daily Ukulele*.
(PHOTO BY ELIZABETH MAIHOCK
BELOFF)

Below: Oasis Ukulele Strummers'
"master at arms," Tony Cappa
with the author. (PHOTO BY
ELIZABETH MAIHOCK BELOFF)

When it was released in 2010, *The Daily Ukulele* quickly found its audience and continues to be our best-selling songbook. Because of its success, there was significant interest in a follow-up. It occurred to me that a leap year could be used to justify another book with, in this case, "366" additional songs. We asked fans of the first book to email us their song preferences for this new volume and we received hundreds of suggestions, many of which we included. In 2012 (a leap year!), we released *The Daily Ukulele: Leap Year Edition — 366 More Great Songs for Better Living.*

One of the artists I was determined to include in this new edition was Todd Rundgren, who was in my pantheon of the all-time greatest songwriters. We chose Todd's novelty song, "Bang the Drum All Day," because he had started performing it on a baritone ukulele after moving to Hawai'i. As we were prepping the song, I thought how great it would be if there was an additional verse that referenced the ukulele. Our friend, Greg Hawkes, a big uke fan and keyboardist for Todd's touring band, put me in touch with Todd's management team. I made my request and waited. At the zero hour, Todd came through with a new special extra verse. It was perfect.

Celebrating Flea Market Music's 25th Anniversary with Hal Leonard executives at the 2017 NAMM. (L-R: Larry Morton, Keith Mardak, the author, Liz, David Jahnke, and Ronny Schiff). (PHOTO BY TRISH DULKA / COURTESY HAL LEONARD)

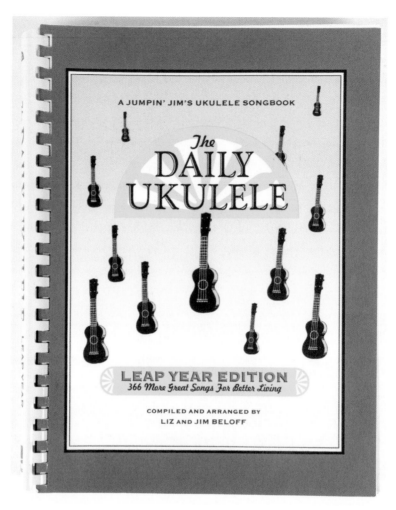

The Daily Ukulele: Leap Year Edition cover. (COURTESY OF FLEA MARKET MUSIC, INC./HAL LEONARD LLC)

Another song in the *Leap Year* edition was "Longing to Belong" by Eddie Vedder. It was included because I'd gotten to know the song and the album it came from quite well. The year before, Eddie, the lead vocalist of the rock band, Pearl Jam, was about to release *Ukulele Songs*, a new solo album, and he wanted to have those songs available in songbook form, similar to our *Jumpin' Jim's* books. I was given the album in advance, so I could determine the chords Ed was playing. Charylu Roberts and Jamison Smeltz joined me to engrave and transcribe the music.

It turned out that Eddie had found inspiration in our early songbooks. In a 2002 interview in *The Ukulele Occasional* magazine, there was this exchange:

EV: There's this guy that puts out the little books.

UO: Jim Beloff?

EV: Yeah, Jumpin' Jim. Sometimes I go through them to find some interesting chords just to start with.

And so, by 2011, Ed was ready to put out an entire ukulele album of his original songs, plus some covers including, "More Than You Know," "Dream a Little Dream of Me," and "Tonight You Belong to Me." Most of the songs were fairly straightforward, but a few featured altered chords that I just couldn't find or reproduce. I needed to see what he was playing. Ed was on tour in Australia at the time, but we would trade emails, and then when I was really stuck, he would film himself playing a passage or specific chord with a GoPro video camera. Two of the how-to-play pages from *The Daily Ukulele* were adapted for the front section of the *Ukulele Songs* songbook and we added our standard chord chart. Next to that, we placed a page of what we called "Ed's Chords" that showcased all of his out-of-the-ordinary chords and fingerings. The limited-edition hardcover version of the book was only available to members of the Pearl Jam fan club and it completely sold out before the book was released.

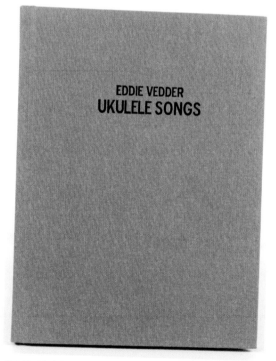

Eddie Vedder Ukulele Songs songbook cover.
(COURTESY OF THE TEN CLUB)

Eddie Vedder with the author and his nephews Ben (left) and Josh Webb (right).
(PHOTO BY ELIZABETH MAIHOCK BELOFF)

After the *Ukulele Songs* album was released, Ed went on a solo tour. We'd never actually met and so when the tour stopped in Hartford, Connecticut, that June, we were given comp tickets and backstage passes. After living in Eddie Vedder–world for half a year, it was great to finally meet the man.

The Daily Ukulele books were all arranged for GCEA-tuned instruments, which was and remains the most popular tuning today. However, as the books became part of the basic repertoire for more and more ukulele clubs, baritone players in those groups felt left out since they were using the lower DGBE tuning. Given that, we released baritone uke versions of both books. In 2015, we published a "portable" version of the first book titled *The Daily Ukulele: To Go!*, which was significantly smaller and lighter.

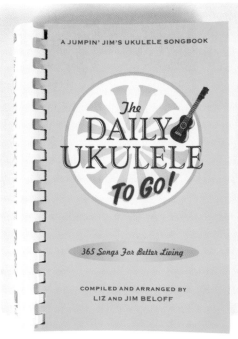

Above: Both *Daily Ukulele for Baritone* Uke Editions covers. (COURTESY OF FLEA MARKET MUSIC, INC./HAL LEONARD LLC)

Left: *The Daily Ukulele to Go!* cover. (COURTESY OF FLEA MARKET MUSIC, INC./HAL LEONARD LLC)

More

In addition to the books, we kept filling the DVD pipeline, too. *The Joy of Uke* instructional video was followed by *The Joy of Uke 2*, which was aimed at intermediate players. Lyle Ritz was my special guest, and at the end of the DVD, Liz and I sang and played our version of "Tonight You Belong to Me," with Lyle nailing a great tenor uke solo. Lyle also made an instructional for Flea Market Music that featured arrangements from *Lyle Lite*, his third *Ukulele Masters* songbook. The DVD, *Lyle's Style*, included an interview with Lyle where we discussed his multifaceted career.

After *The Daily Ukulele* songbook came out, we taped *Jumpin' Jim's Ukulele Workshop* in Woodstock, New York, the actual "home" of Homespun Video. For that DVD, I taught twelve songs from *The Daily Ukulele* with a lot of the techniques and "teachable moments" that I typically shared in my workshops. A circle of sorts closed when John Sebastian, who lived in the area, backed me up on guitar as I strummed and sang his Lovin' Spoonful classic, "Daydream." It was thirteen years after we had first met at NAMM and talked about how "Daydream" was such a natural uke song.

The Joy of Uke 2 cover.
(COURTESY OF HOMESPUN VIDEO)

Jumpin' Jim's Ukulele Workshop cover.
(COURTESY OF HOMESPUN VIDEO)

Left: *Lyle's Style* cover.
(COURTESY OF FLEA MARKET MUSIC, INC.)

Below: John Sebastian with the author during the taping of *Jumpin' Jim's Ukulele Workshop*.
(PHOTO BY ELIZABETH MAIHOCK BELOFF)

Media coverage kept on rolling in, as well. Big comprehensive articles in magazines like *Business 2.0*, "My Sweet Embraceable Uke" (the puns kept on coming in, too),
and *Hawai'i Magazine*, "Strumming in Style," continued to advance the idea of a new
"third wave" of popularity. In "Fountain of Uke" (more puns!) from the April 23, 2002,
issue of the *San Francisco Examiner*, writer Toni Logan set up the sorry state of affairs
following the Tiny Tim era and then pivoted:

> But now the ukulele is surfing its third wave of popularity on the mainland.
> From a traveling museum exhibit titled "Ukulele Fever," now showing at the
> Stamford Museum in Stamford, Connecticut, to this weekend's shindig in
> Hayward, the uke is taking center stage and finally regaining respect. The
> current uke trend started in the early 1990s and steadily gathered heat. Jim
> Beloff, a former ad salesman for *Billboard* magazine, helped set the ball rolling.
> An amateur musician, he bought his first uke, a vintage Martin, in 1992 at
> the Rose Bowl flea market in Pasadena. "I think what's driving this renewed
> interest is that we are all seeking our inner Hawai'i," Beloff muses. "The uke
> provides downtime and a vacation in lieu of traveling to the islands."

Also in 2002, on October 1 in the *Los Angeles Times*, Kim Murphy wrote a piece
titled "Ukulele Strikes a New Chord." It mentioned that we had sold out our latest
UKEtopia show at McCabe's, an evening of ukulele gospel titled "O Strummer, Where
Art Thou?" The article pointed out that the ukulele was now "hip" in Hawai'i and
had attracted a new generation of players like twenty-five-year-old Jake Shimabukuro
"whose intense, whirlwind strumming has been compared to Hendrix's."

After six years, the uke history book was rereleased in a revised and expanded edition. Reversing the usual rollout, Backbeat, our publisher, green-lighted a hardcover
for this edition and even added a cloth edging that resembled Hawaiian shirt fabric. In
the new introduction, I wrote:

> When the first edition of *The Ukulele—A Visual History* was published in 1997,
> the ukulele was just beginning to appear again on the pop culture radar. . . .
> Six years later, I'm happy to report that the ukulele is in the midst of a genuine

renaissance, a true third wave of popularity. Ukulele festivals are happening all over the Mainland, songbooks for the ukulele are once again plentiful, fine new ukulele luthiers are setting up shops throughout Hawai'i and the Mainland, and a whole new crop of uke artists and virtuosos are filling concert halls and selling their CDs. For ukulele players, these are exciting times.

This new edition of *The Ukulele—A Visual History* is a chance to improve upon the first edition in three primary ways. Thanks especially to Hawaiian music historian, John King, we've made some small but critical changes to the first edition text regarding the Portuguese ancestor of the ukulele and its earliest days after arriving in Hawai'i. The principal change is referring to the Madeiran instrument as the machete rather than the original, braguinha. Secondly, it was a chance to include information about new players, new uke makers, new books and periodicals as well as recent pop culture visibility. It was also an opportunity to include some of the fascinating history behind the ukulele in Japan and Canada. Finally, here was an excuse to include more images of fun and unique vintage ukes.

For the layout of the revised edition, I worked closely with graphic designer Doug Haverty, another friend from my *Billboard* days. In a new closing chapter, I included short bios of new generation players like Jake Shimabukuro, Daniel Ho, Herb Ohta Jr. (Herb Ohta's son), John King, Janet Klein, Azo Bell from Australia, The Langley Ukulele Ensemble and James Hill from Canada, The Ukulele Club de Paris from France, and Iwao from Japan. I also wanted to acknowledge some additional veteran players including Byron Yasui, Gordon Marks and Benny Chong from Hawai'i, Travis Harrelson, and, especially, Bill Tapia.

The Ukulele—A Visual History revised hardcover edition cover. (COURTESY OF BACK-BEAT BOOKS, ROWMAN & LITTLEFIELD PUBLISHING GROUP, INC. AND GLOBE PEQUOT PRESS.)

The author with Jake Shimabukuro. (PHOTO BY ELIZABETH MAIHOCK BELOFF)

Bill landed on the ukulele scene like a meteorite. It was 2001 and he was ninety-three years old. Bill's backstory became the stuff of legend. Born on New Year's Day, 1908, in Honolulu (amazingly, his mother, father, and aunt were also born on January 1), Bill picked up the ukulele at the age of seven and soon was earning money playing for tips at USO (United Service Organizations) shows for World War I troops and later on, on cruise ships. In 1927, he played at the opening of the famously pink, Royal Hawaiian Hotel in Waikiki as part of Johnny Noble's band. He also gave uke lessons to visiting celebrities like Shirley Temple, Jimmy Durante, Clark Gable, and even Arthur Godfrey.

Eventually, Bill moved to the San Francisco area where he became known as a jazz guitarist, doing studio work, teaching, and sitting in with big-name musicians like Louis Armstrong, Billie Holiday, and Bing Crosby. He married and had a daughter and pretty much stopped playing the ukulele for fifty years. In his early nineties, he moved near Los Angeles to be closer to family. At a local music store, he strummed a ukulele and learned that the instrument was enjoying a resurgence of popularity. That led Bill to us.

Bill was a natural storyteller and could recall everything from his long life. When we first met, out of curiosity, I asked him if he knew Sonny Cunha, Rick's grandfather who passed away years before Rick was born. Bill said, "Sure I knew him! Big guy, funny guy!" I couldn't wait to introduce Bill to Rick. Imagine meeting someone in midlife, who knew your grandfather. Like many others who met Bill, Liz and I felt compelled to formally interview him, which we did at his home in Westminster, California. He was always a sharp dresser and he looked especially dapper the day we videotaped him, sharing some colorful episodes of his life. After the interview, he said he had another appointment, and as we headed to our car, we watched Bill hop into his car and zoom off. On the cover of his *Duke of Uke* album, Bill is pictured sitting in his custom PT Cruiser.

One of our favorite Bill stories happened at the 2002 UKEtopia concert. By now, Bill was a regular member of the show and he was slotted to play first. Just before the show, we learned that he had fallen and fractured his wrist. We were stunned by the news, but quickly shuffled the set list and carried on. Twenty minutes later, Bill showed up backstage with his entourage, his arm in a cast and a sling, and determined to play. I went on stage to announce that, miraculously, Bill Tapia was in the house after all and, despite his injury, eager to perform. Bill walked out to a hero's welcome. He performed four songs with the cast on and the audience went wild.

If they're fortunate, at some point in their career, an artist will arrive at that moment where they're hitting on all cylinders—creatively, as well as commercially. Incredibly, for Bill, it happened in his mid- to late nineties. He was feted in the press, got a record deal, got an agent and publicist, had documentaries made about

Bill Tapia. (PHOTO BY ELIZABETH MAIHOCK BELOFF)

UKEtopia poster designed by Liz Beloff. (PHOTO BY JOHN GIAMMATTEO)

him, toured constantly, and was inducted into the Ukulele Hall of Fame. Bill celebrated his one-hundredth birthday with a big concert at the Warner Grand Theater in San Pedro, California. The year before, at ninety-nine years old, he bought a townhouse in Makaha Valley, Hawai'i, with 20 percent down and a thirty-year fixed-rate mortgage. Just another example of the extraordinary spirit that was Bill Tapia.

Our UKEtopia shows at McCabe's continued on annually through 2005, at which point we moved to Connecticut. Guest solo artists and groups appearing in the show included Peter Brooke Turner from the Ukulele Orchestra of Great Britain, Ritt Henn, Waste of Aces, Charlie Oyama, Bergman Broom, The UKEdelics, The Acres, Nancy Felixson, Shorty Long, Dan Sawyer, Michelle Kiba, Steve Rose, Sid Hausman, and Eddie Montana.

Sales of Fluke ukuleles also reflected the surge of interest in the instrument. By April 2001, five thousand Flukes had been sold. Dale and Phyllis had moved the business out of their basement and into an old former gas station near their home in New Hartford, Connecticut. With a small team, they oversaw the many steps involved in assembling, marketing, and distributing the Fluke ukes and developed new designs, such as the cow print, "Moo-kulele." Liz came up with their business name, The Magic Fluke Company, as well as several soundboard designs.

Dale in the basement where Fluke ukuleles were first manufactured. (PHOTO BY ELIZABETH MAIHOCK BELOFF)

Above: Phyllis and Dale Webb, the author, and Liz at NAMM. (AUTHOR'S COLLECTION)

Left: The first numbered Fluke. (FROM THE COLLECTION OF FLEA MARKET MUSIC)

Right: The "Pool" Fluke with soundboard designed by Liz. (FROM THE COLLECTION OF FLEA MARKET MUSIC)

By this time, the word was out about the big warm tone and cool appearance of the Fluke. As one fan said, "It's got a great, resonant sound, stays in tune and it's as cute as a chipmunk. The iMac or VW Beetle of ukes! A terrific, affordable product." In 2002, The Magic Fluke Company, introduced the smaller, soprano-scale, "Flea" ukulele with a more traditional rounded pineapple shape. Again, named by Liz, this new uke was originally designed for younger players, but quickly became popular with adults, as well. Like the Fluke, it could stand up on its end, but the back-shell was a bit flatter. Flukes and Fleas also earned another reputation. They were surprisingly durable. Boaters would write in about how their Fluke accidentally fell into the ocean and survived just fine.

Over the years, The Magic Fluke Company, has added the "Firefly" banjo-uke, "Timber" short-scale bass uke, and "Cricket," travel violin to their offerings. The factory is now in a beautiful solar-powered, timber-framed building on the main street into Sheffield, Massachusetts, at the southern end of the Berkshire Mountains. As of 2020, they had built and shipped over seventy-thousand USA-made instruments.

Left: The "Uke Can Change the World" Flea with soundboard designed by Liz. (FROM THE COLLECTION OF FLEA MARKET MUSIC)

Right: The limited edition "Fleamingo" Flea with soundboard designed by Liz. (FROM THE COLLECTION OF FLEA MARKET MUSIC)

Dale and Phyllis Webb and Flukes at the Magic Fluke Company in 2020. (PHOTO BY
HARRY LEVENSTEIN / COURTESY THE MAGIC FLUKE COMPANY)

The Magic Fluke Company sign. (PHOTO BY HARRY LEVENSTEIN / COURTESY THE MAGIC FLUKE
COMPANY)

Above: Flea ukuleles ready to go. (PHOTO BY HARRY LEVENSTEIN / COURTESY THE MAGIC FLUKE COMPANY)

Left: "Firefly" banjo uke. (PHOTO BY HARRY LEVENSTEIN / COURTESY THE MAGIC FLUKE COMPANY)

Right: The "Timber" bass. (PHOTO BY HARRY LEVENSTEIN / COURTESY THE MAGIC FLUKE COMPANY)

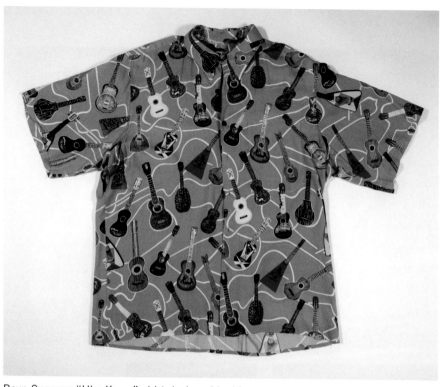

Reyn Spooner "Uke Krazy" shirt designed by Liz. (PHOTO BY JOHN GIAMMATTEO)

MDHF catalog, Summer 2000. (COURTESY OF FLEA MARKET MUSIC, INC.)

Twice a year, our *MDHF* catalog detailed all of the various new designs and options, available on the Fluke and Flea ukes. We also added other kinds of uke-related items. In the same summer 2002 catalog where the Flea debuted, we offered Jake Shimabukuro's first solo CD, *Sunday Morning*. We also advertised the "Uke Krazy" Hawaiian shirt, designed by Liz in collaboration with the Hawaiian shirtmaker, Reyn Spooner. At the time, Reyn Spooner was still owned and operated by the original family, and manufacturing was done on the Big Island of Hawai'i. Because we had shown that we could sell dozens of pricey Hawaiian shirts with a ukulele theme, Reyn Spooner invited Liz to design "Uke Krazy," which featured some of our favorite novelty ukes plus a Fluke on a Googie-inspired background. The shirts came in all sizes and several colors including mint green. The entire run sold out quickly.

My dad, Marvin, had always been a big supporter of everything my sister, Phyllis, and I did. When the Fluke came out, he cajoled two of his closest friends, Bruce Burchsted and Peter Burch, into learning how to play them. After a while, they had a few dozen songs mastered and in March 2000, they entertained at a private party. That was the *humble* beginning of a run of over four hundred performances as The Humble Bees. Playing an average of thirty-plus gigs a year, mostly at senior centers, churches, and nursing homes, they raised over $35,000 in scholarship money for the AAUW (American Association of University Women).

The Humblebees in Vermont, April 2003. (L-R: Marvin Beloff, Peter Burch, and Bruce Burchsted). (PHOTO BY ELIZABETH MAIHOCK BELOFF)

After "Ukulele Fever," we worked with three other California museums to mount their own ukulele exhibitions. On May 21, 2005, the "History of the Ukulele" opened at the International Surfing Museum in Huntington Beach. "Strings of Paradise," a tribute to the ukulele and steel guitar opened on May 26, 2007, at The Fullerton Museum Center, and the NAMM museum, The Museum of Making Music, opened "The Ukulele & You," on August 11, 2007. Subtitled, "America's Enduring Love of the Jumping Flea," and based at NAMM headquarters in Carlsbad, California, it was a "special exhibition dedicated to the history of Hawai'i's versatile instrument." Liz and I served as cocurators along with several other experts, including Rick Turner, Fred Fallin, and Andy Andrews. The exhibit featured over two hundred instruments drawn from private collections, including our own. The museum put together a busy schedule of receptions, concerts, workshops, and discussions throughout the run of the show which closed at the end of January 2008.

As the third wave grew, ukulele festivals began to sprout up all across the United States and internationally. We were invited to teach and perform at many of them. One of the biggest was the Southern California Ukulele Festival, which attracted well over a thousand attendees. In 2004, Festival Director, Susan McCormick, asked me to write a theme song for the fest. While ruminating on a possible title, I thought about how often people would say, "You can't help but smile when you see a ukulele." That led to "Can't Help But Smile," which Susan adopted as the festival song and, with a rewrite of the verses, became a kind of ukulele theme song for Liz and me. It's also become the theme song for ukulele clubs. Here are the lyrics to the first verse and chorus:

It's no secret that we love the ukulele,

It is a passion,

We can't deny.

And the reason's clearly written on our faces,

And we'd be happy,

To tell you why.

Can't help but smile,

Can't help but smile,

When we play the ukulele,

Can't help but smile.

Can't help but sing,

Can't help but strum,

Can't help but feel like we're on some Hawaiian isle.

So fine,

So fun,

When we all play together as one.

And life is good,

For a while,

Can't help but sing,

Can't help but strum,

Can't help but smile!

31st Annual Ukulele Festival, Honolulu, Hawai'i.
(PHOTO BY ELIZABETH MAIHOCK BELOFF)

Various uke fest T-shirts. (PHOTO BY JOHN GIAMMATTEO)

The author leading a workshop at McCabe's Guitar Shop. (PHOTO BY ELIZABETH MAIHOCK BELOFF)

Above: A workshop at McCabe's Guitar Shop. (PHOTO BY ELIZABETH MAIHOCK BELOFF)

Left: A workshop at Giacoletti Music store. (PHOTO BY ELIZABETH MAIHOCK BELOFF)

House of Musical Traditions workshop. (PHOTO BY ELIZABETH MAIHOCK BELOFF)

NAMM Museum of Making Music workshop. (PHOTO BY ELIZABETH MAIHOCK BELOFF)

The author with Liz outside the Corktown Ukulele Jam in Toronto, Ontario. (AUTHOR'S COLLECTION)

In addition to California, we attended uke fests, gave workshops, and performed in Connecticut, Florida, Hawai'i, Illinois, Indiana, Maine, Maryland, Massachusetts, Michigan, Minnesota, New Jersey, New Mexico, New York, Nevada, North Carolina, Oregon, Pennsylvania, Rhode Island, Vermont, Virginia, Washington, and Wisconsin. In Canada, we taught and performed in Port Dover and Toronto, Ontario, and Portage la Prairie, Manitoba.

The author with Liz at Proctor's in Schenectady, New York. (PHOTO BY JOEL ECKHAUS)

The author and Liz with Bruce Belland of the Four Preps and Spencer Davis of the Spencer Davis Group on Catalina in 2005. (AUTHOR'S COLLECTION)

In 2009, we ventured to another faraway place—Australia. John Chandler, an avid uke fan and instructor in Sydney, reached out by email offering to arrange a tour for Liz and me through much of the eastern coast of the continent. John had a wholesale import and distribution business selling ukuleles to music stores down under and had also founded SSCUM (St. George and Sutherland Community of Ukulele Musicians), the first uke club in Sydney and the second one in all of Australia. Today, there are dozens of ukulele clubs in Sydney alone. It was a leap of faith for us, but all the emailing back and forth with John inspired confidence. When we finally met John and his wife, Evelyn, they seemed like old friends.

After the four of us spent a few days sightseeing in Auckland and around Rotorua, New Zealand, we flew to Sydney where we stayed in John and Evelyn's home, while I gave workshops at the various uke clubs around Sydney. Participating in social clubs is very much a way of life in Australia, and the country seemed to be especially receptive to the combination of strumming, singing, socializing, eating, and drinking that came with being in a ukulele club. We also gave workshops and performed in Canberra, Bangalow, and Melbourne. A high point in Byron Bay was spending some time at the home of Azo Bell, a virtuoso player with his own distinctive technique and sound.

In Melbourne, we were guests of the Melbourne Ukulele Kollective, where we gave a workshop and performed. While there, we also caught up with our old pal Chuck Fayne and his wife, Hilda. A strange coincidence occurred at the Queen Victoria Market. As we were walking around the many stalls of exotic fish and meats, we passed by a chemist [drugstore] with inexpensive ukuleles for sale along with the typical display of medications. It was enough of an unexpected pairing that Liz stopped to ask about it. The owner, John Hurlston, was summoned and he was stunned to see me there. We had never met, nor did he know I was in the country, but he swore that he had planned to reach out to me that very day via email to ask my advice regarding his collection of vintage ukes. And there I was, standing in front of him.

The author and Liz at the Sydney Opera House, 2009. (PHOTO BY JOHN CHANDLER)

Workshop in Canberra. (PHOTO BY ELIZABETH MAIHOCK BELOFF)

Workshop at the Balmain Ukulele Klub in Sydney. (PHOTO BY JOHN CHANDLER)

John Hurlston and the author at the Queen Victoria Market in Melbourne. (PHOTO BY ELIZABETH MAIHOCK BELOFF)

The author, Liz, and Evelyn and John Chandler with the Fab 4 in Liverpool, England, 2019. (AUTHOR'S COLLECTION)

We were invited to Perth, on the western side of Australia, by Lionel Cranfield of Zenith Music, a longtime music retailer whom we had gotten to know through the NAMM shows. Lionel showed us around Perth for a couple of days and then we gave a workshop and performance at his store. From Perth, we flew back to Sydney and then the next day, Thanksgiving, we flew from Sydney to Los Angeles, and then on to New York. Because of the time change, we were served Thanksgiving dinner twice. The Australia trip paid yet another dividend. Ever since, John, Evelyn, Liz, and I have continued to travel together—to Greece, Turkey, Ireland, Wales, and England, and always with ukes in tow.

As part of a trip to Spain and Portugal in 2017, Liz and I decided to include a two-day visit to Madeira, the ancestral home of the modern-day ukulele. A ninety-minute flight from Lisbon, Madeira is situated in the Atlantic Ocean southwest of Portugal. The overall population is a bit more than 250,000 and its seaside capital is Funchal. Madeira is also known for its spectacular beauty, New Year's Eve fireworks, and wine.

In 1879, however, poverty and overpopulation on the island forced some Madeirans to seek employment in the Hawaiian sugarcane fields. It was a four-month voyage, and after the *Ravenscrag* sailed into Honolulu harbor, one of the passengers jumped onto the wharf to sing a song of thanksgiving for their safe arrival. What attracted the attention of the curious Hawaiians was the unusual musical instrument he was playing— a small four-stringed, Madeiran wooden instrument called a machete. The machete, along with the tuning of the rajão, a five-stringed Madeiran instrument, eventually evolved into the modern-day ukulele.

The rajão was the instrument we encountered on our first night in Madeira. After dinner, we heard folk music in the old town area of Funchal, where many restaurants are located. We followed the sound and discovered a group of six strolling musicians. As I watched the rajão players, I noticed that the chord fingerings they were using looked familiar. After listening a bit and talking to one of the musicians who spoke some English, I was invited to play a rajão with the group. The song was a simple three-chord, folk tune. As I played along, I couldn't help thinking about the mash-up of cultures in 1879 that led to this momentary musical exchange 138 years later. Afterward, we all introduced ourselves and I bought one of their handmade traditional pointy hats.

The author with folk musicians in Madeira, 2017. (PHOTO BY ELIZABETH MAIHOCK BELOFF)

Mighty Uke, the first feature-length documentary about the ukulele's third wave, premiered at the Woodstock Film festival in 2009. Filmmakers Tony Coleman and Margaret Meagher traveled the globe to capture the worldwide phenomenon with stops in California, London, Tel Aviv, Tokyo, and, of course, Hawai'i. They also spent time with Liz and me in our Connecticut home. In a segment preceded by a title card that read: "So how did this ukulele revival happen?," we shared our Rose Bowl origin story and then we did a reenactment of sorts, filmed at the Antiques Garage Flea Market on 25th Street in New York City, a few blocks from our former loft.

Mighty Uke DVD cover.
(COURTESY OF TINY GOAT FILMS LTD.)

LIZ, JAMES HILL, AND MIGHTY UKE FILMMAKERS, MARGARET MEAGHER AND TONY COLEMAN. (PHOTO BY JIM BELOFF)

Other books about the history of the ukulele made their way to store shelves. *Ukulele*, by Daniel Dixon with Dixie Dixon and Jayne McKay was subtitled, *The World's Friendliest Instrument*, and included a chapter on Liz and me. Daniel was the son of painter Maynard Dixon and photographer Dorothea Lange, and *Ukulele*, published in 2011, was his love letter to the instrument. Ian Whitcomb's *Ukulele Heroes* celebrated all of the legendary players as well as his own long history with the instrument and our UKEtopia shows. Despite all of this activity, there was still room for a deep-dive, scholarly work. *The 'Ukulele: A History*, by John King and Jim Tranquada, was researched over many years and published by the University of Hawai'i Press in 2012. I was honored to provide a back-cover quote which included, "Here at last, is the complete story of the 'ukulele."

With all of the new interest in the ukulele, it was only a question of time before there was an American magazine dedicated to the subject. In October 2012, Stringletter Media published the premiere issue of *Ukulele* with a rare Martin 5K tenor ukulele and Jake Shimabukuro on the cover. Inside was a review of the Fluke. With the spring 2013 issue, *Ukulele* began its current quarterly frequency with a story titled, "Uke

Entrepreneur" by Jeffrey Pepper Rodgers about me and Flea Market Music, Inc. My "Jammin' with Jumpin' Jim" column also ran in the magazine for several years and covered many favorite ukulele tips and techniques.

Although my serious collecting days are long behind me, I still keep an eye out for interesting ukuleles and collectibles. The biggest acquisition I've made in the last few years was a late 1920s Martin 5K in pristine condition. The 5K was the most ornate of the Martin line and is considered one of the holiest of "holy grail" vintage ukes. Only 727 were made, virtually all before 1945. I wasn't looking for one, but I also knew that I'd probably never have another chance at one again, so I pulled the trigger. It joins several dozen others that are mostly novelty ukes with canoeists, cheerleaders, cowboys, dice, dominoes, playing cards, pyramids, and cartoons of Betty Boop and Harold Teen on them. The most cherished uke in the collection was a gift from Lyle Ritz—the Gibson tenor cutaway pictured on the cover of *How About Uke* and played on both Verve albums.

Some of my favorites ukes are pictured here:

Lyle Ritz's Gibson tenor cutaway.
(PHOTO BY JOHN GIAMMATTEO)

Gibson "Poinsettia" uke (front and back). (PHOTO BY JOHN GIAMMATTEO)

Martin 5K uke.
(PHOTO BY JOHN GIAMMATTEO)

Lyon & Healy "Shrine" uke.
(PHOTO BY JOHN GIAMMATTEO)

National Model 2 uke.

(PHOTO BY JOHN GIAMMATTEO)

"Sweetheart" uke.

(PHOTO BY JOHN GIAMMATTEO)

"Jungle" uke.
(PHOTO BY JOHN GIAMMATTEO)

"Cheerleader" uke.
(PHOTO BY JOHN GIAMMATTEO)

"Betty Boop" uke.

(PHOTO BY JOHN GIAMMATTEO)

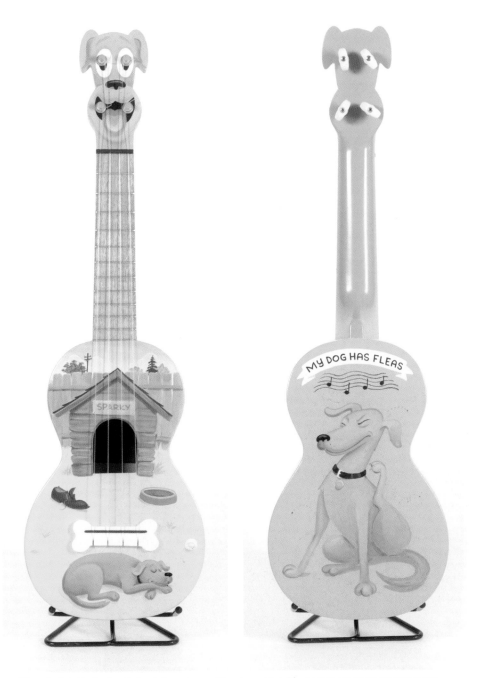

"Poochalele" uke by Robert Armstrong (front and back). (PHOTO BY JOHN GIAMMATTEO)

The Songs

Promoting the ukulele in so many different ways and places has been thrilling and fascinating. I never imagined I would publish songbooks, write a history of anything, or be on the same stage with a symphony orchestra performing a work of mine. Ditto for consulting on a museum show or performing in Japan and Australia. Or certainly writing this book. Mostly, I never dreamed Liz and I would be credited with helping to repopularize a musical instrument. And yet, as fulfilling as all that has been, I'm reminded that it all happened in the wake of discovering that the ukulele was my ideal songwriting companion. For me, it's still about the songs.

Thankfully, in between everything else, the songwriting has continued. My collaboration with Herb Ohta has been especially fruitful. We've written over fifty songs together, five just in 2020. In 2004, Flea Market Music released *The Finer Things*, an album of sixteen of the songs, performed by top studio musicians and ten vocalists. The album was produced by Rick Cunha, Jim Hughart, and me, and featured Hal Blaine on drums; Lyle Ritz, Jim Hughart, and Simeon Pillich on acoustic bass; and Ed Vodicka on

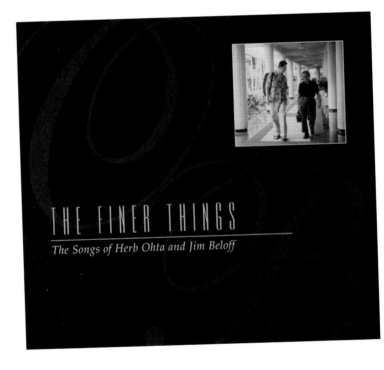

Jim Beloff: The Finer Things CD cover. (COURTESY OF FLEA MARKET MUSIC, INC.)

THE FINER THINGS

The Songs of Herb Ohta and Jim Beloff

Above: *The Finer Things* Los Angeles session musicians. (L-R: Ed Vodicka, the author, Lyle Ritz, Jim Hughart, Hal Blaine, Frank Marocco, and Rick Cunha). (PHOTO BY ELIZABETH MAIHOCK BELOFF)

Left: Herb Ohta during *The Finer Things* Hawai'i sessions. (PHOTO BY ELIZABETH MAIHOCK BELOFF)

piano. Herb and Lyle played ukulele on several of the songs and the great accordionist, Frank Marocco played on two of the tracks. Six of the songs, "Rainforest Waltz," "Blues on a Ukulele," "The French Café," "Soup du Jour," "The Hawaiian Turnaround," and "Closer to the Light," have been covered by other artists including, Lyle Ritz, Seaman Dan, Victoria Vox, Cali Rose, Ginai, and Cathy Fink and Marcy Marxer.

The Finer Things also included a song, "At the Magic Laundromat," sung by the actor, William H. Macy. We met Bill on the set of *Jurassic Park III* at the end of 2000. Sam Neill was in the film and they got to talking about ukuleles and our songbooks. A hometown friend, Bruce Donnellan, was the special effects foreman on the movie, and he arranged the meeting. It turned out that Bill had picked up the ukulele a few years earlier and had our songbooks. Not long after that first meeting, Bill started hiring me to write songs for special occasions. The first one was for a surprise birthday party for his wife, Felicity Huffman. Another one was written for Bill to perform at a fundraiser for his longtime friend and playwright, David Mamet. Like the song for Felicity, Bill would load me up with information about the honoree and I would mold that into something he could sing and play. In most cases, these tributes needed to be written in a hurry and the challenge of taking a lot of raw material and fashioning it quickly into something worthy of the subject appealed to me. Bill called after the David Mamet gala to report that the audience "ate their young." I think that meant the song went over well.

In 2003, Bill asked me to write a song for his character in the Showtime miniseries, *Out of Order*. He played a burned-out movie producer with a drinking problem. He was on location and needed the song the next day. Twenty-four hours later, I emailed "I Don't Want to Drink Alone," along with the chords and a basic recording of me singing the song. Bill performed most of it in the scene and then a recording of the whole song was added to the credit roll at the end of that episode.

Later that same year, Bill asked me to write a song that he and Felicity could sing at a benefit for the National Breast Cancer Coalition Fund. With encouragement from Bill, I wrote "Are They Real," which dealt with Hollywood's obsession with breasts. As we rehearsed the number, Bill and Felicity decided it would be fun to have Liz and me sing it with them. It was a star-studded evening and Liz shared a dressing room with Rita Wilson, Tom Hank's wife. We also hit it off with the director of the benefit, Stuart

Ross, who had written the long-running, off-Broadway musical, *Forever Plaid*. Later on, Stuart would play an important role in another song of mine.

Bill also called me in 2006 from the set of *Wild Hogs*, the motorcycle buddy movie he was shooting with John Travolta, Martin Lawrence, and Tim Allen. It looked like there was a chance he might be able to strum a song in a campfire scene. Once again, I had one day to come up with something that would be appropriate for the moment. That led to "The Open Road," which, sadly, did not make it into the film. That wasn't the end of it, though. Just before the movie's release in March 2007, the four principals were set to appear on "The Oprah Winfrey Show." Bill had called me the day before to see if I could come up with a comic song about how he was the coolest dude in the movie. And, he wanted the lyrics to dis the three other stars . . . in good fun, of course. Because he would have little time to rehearse, I decided to recycle the melody to the Felicity birthday song that he already knew. Here is the lyric:

If you're into motorcycles,
Do what all the bikers do,
Rent that movie *Easy Rider*,
Wild Hogs is not for you.
John Travolta isn't sexy,
Martin Lawrence isn't tough,
Mister Allen isn't funny,
Only Macy's got the stuff,
Laugh if you like,
But I look good on my bike.

Man, I look mean, in *Wild Hogs*.
On my machine, in *Wild Hogs*,
Oh boy, this boy can ride.
I've got it all together when,
I'm all zipped up in leather, I,
Really look good in hide.
Johnny, go back to school,

Martin, you're Big Mama's fool,

And, Tim, you're just a tool!

You think you've got velocity,

But I got Felicity,

I'm the only one that's cool!

(I'll say it again . . .)

I'm the only one that's cool!

As I was racing the clock to pull this together, Liz came up with the killer penultimate line, "You think you've got velocity, / But I got Felicity." Bill nailed the performance (on his Flea uke no less) and after he finished, Travolta, Allen, and Lawrence got up from the couch and pretended to beat him up. As the credits rolled Bill did a shout-out to me for writing the song. The postscript to the *Wild Hogs* story is that Liz suggested we start singing "The Open Road" in our gigs. It became an audience favorite and I enjoyed sharing the story of its birth.

The author with William H. Macy on the set of *Jurassic Park III*. (PHOTO BY ELIZABETH MAI-HOCK BELOFF)

Another collaboration with Bill happened in 2017. He needed a song for a sex scene in *The Layover*, a comedy he was directing. The one-minute scene included brief nudity mixed in with a good bit of furniture wrecking and Bill wanted a song that would lighten the mood. Once again, he needed the song right away. Over the years, I've had some success working on creative problems in my sleep. The next morning, I woke up with a title, "This Could Be My Lucky Day," and much of the lyrics. Bill put together a minute-long a cappella version of the song and I was happy to see that it lightened the scene just as he hoped.

An opportunity to write a song for the CBS series *JAG* came along in 2002. The episode was built around a World War II flashback and the creative team planned to have a member of the cast sing and strum a well-known, 1940s-era *hapa haole* song. The "sync-rights," however, were enormously expensive and they approached me for a recommendation of a public domain song that might work instead. After exploring some possibilities, we all agreed that nothing before 1923 would work quite as well. At that point, I offered to write a song that would sound period-appropriate. Only a verse or two of "That Hawaiian Melody" ended up in "Each of Us Angels" from Season 8, but the full version of the song has had a long afterlife. It's been covered by Michelle Kiba and Tripping Lily and there are many other renditions on YouTube.

Just before we moved from Los Angeles to Connecticut in 2005, I was contacted by an assistant to Bette Midler to see if I could give Bette ukulele lessons. Bette had grown up in Hawai'i and felt it was time she learned how to play her native instrument. I didn't give private ukulele lessons, but for Bette, I did. She was a great student and after a few lessons, she knew enough to progress on her own. During our last lesson, Bette sang and strummed the Beatles "With a Little Help from My Friends," from the *'60s Uke-In* songbook. While being serenaded, it was hard not to think that I was getting a private concert by one of the world's great singers. At the same time, it reminded me of when I was learning the guitar and the sense of accomplishment I felt, the first time I played through the Peter, Paul & Mary hit, "500 Miles." Being able to change the chords as the melody and lyrics unspooled was such a profound moment that I still remember it more than fifty years later.

We stayed in touch with Bette after we moved to Connecticut and in 2007, she invited me to back her up on ukulele at a memorial tribute/concert to Ahmet Ertegun, the cofounder of Atlantic Records, Bette's first label home. The all-star event was held at the Jazz at Lincoln Center's Rose Theater. Bette had decided to honor Ahmet with the Harry Owens, *hapa haole* classic, "Princess Poo-Poo-Ly Has Plenty Pa-Pa-Ya." As Bette and I were waiting in the wings to go on, the stage manager pointed out where on the stage we needed to go. Bette would need to stand where Henry Kissinger was, and I needed to be in the same spot where Eric Clapton was standing. Wow!

The day before the concert, Liz and I met Bette at her New York triplex to rehearse. While we were there, I played "A Ukulele and You," a song I'd written that was inspired by an interview she'd given while on tour in Australia:

Kerry O'Brien: You said you don't want to die on stage and be left clinging to the shards of fame and glory. At the same time, you said other countries—in other countries you are allowed to sing and play music until you die and you don't have to look good doing it.

Bette Midler: That's right. I think my small room with my small combo is coming. I'm learning the piano and I'm also learning the ukulele. And if push comes to shove, I will be out there with that ukulele all by myself and the hell with the rest of them.

Here's the lyric to the first verse and chorus:

Boy I love a big band,
'specially when it swings,
Orchestras are thrilling,
Love to hear those strings.
Love to sing for thousands,
In a concert hall.
But lately I've been thinking,
What's the harm in thinking small . . .

Give me a ukulele and you,

A ukulele and you,

Just give me a uke,

And a song to sing,

And you to sing it to.

A ukulele and you,

No big hullabaloo,

When push comes to shove,

You know what I love?

A ukulele and you.

"Bette Midler: The Showgirl Must Go On" opened in February 2008 at The Colosseum at Caesars Palace in Las Vegas. For the show, Bette asked me to arrange "The Glory of Love" for her to strum and sing onstage. The ukulele she played was a custom-designed "Pineapple" Flea with Swarovski crystals encrusted on the soundboard. They were also available in the gift shop for $3,000.

The author with Liz and Bette Midler in 2007. (AUTHOR'S COLLECTION)

$3,000 Flea ukes with Swarovski crystals in the Bette Midler Gift Shop at Caesars Palace. (PHOTO BY ELIZABETH MAIHOCK BELOFF)

After we got to know Stuart Ross, the director of the breast cancer benefit, I gave him copies of *For the Love of Uke* and *The Finer Things*. Stuart thought his good friend, contemporary folk musician, and songwriter Christine Lavin, might like them, so he forwarded a copy of each to her. Four years later, in 2008, Christine played them and emailed me to say how much she loved my song "Charles Ives." The thing about Christine is that if she loves a song, she'll do whatever she can to spread the word. And so, she spread the word to many of her well-known singer-songwriter friends. A decade later, I heard from Noel Paul Stookey (*aka* Paul of Peter, Paul & Mary), who had learned about the song from Christine and had decided to add it to his repertoire. On April 7, 2018, Liz and I attended a Peter Yarrow & Noel Paul Stookey concert at the Tarrytown Music Hall in New York. To hear Noel, a brilliant songwriter himself, who cowrote several of Peter, Paul & Mary's hits like "I Dig Rock and Roll Music," and also wrote the "Wedding Song (There Is Love)," sing "Charles Ives," was a deeply moving experience for me. The fourteen-year-long word-of-mouth journey was worth the wait.

Liz, Noel Paul Stookey, and the author backstage at the Tarrytown Music Hall in 2018. (AUTHOR'S COLLECTION)

Since the 1999 premiere, I've performed *Uke Can't Be Serious* many times with Phil Ventre conducting the Wallingford Symphony as well as the Choate Symphony Orchestra on tour in Germany and Austria. I also performed it with the Santa Monica High School Orchestra and the Michigan Philharmonic under the baton of Nan Washburn. In 2015, I had the orchestral part rewritten for string quartet, which has allowed me to perform it at several uke fests.

Phil Ventre commissioned me to write another concerto in 2016, which became *The Dove Tale*. Our home on the Connecticut shoreline is near a bird sanctuary and I became intrigued with the mourning dove call, which is particularly melodic, complex, and melancholy. It begged to be musicalized. Once I placed the birdcall at the top of the piece, a narrative began to suggest itself. Jason Nyberg wrote the stirring orchestrations and the piece premiered on October 15, 2017, with Phil conducting the Wallingford Symphony. In 2018, we released, *Two Ukulele Concertos*, an EP that included both *Uke Can't Be Serious* and *The Dove Tale*, plus a recording of "Charles Ives," with additional strings added to Rick Cunha's arrangement.

Performance of *Uke Can't Be Serious* with The Michigan Philharmonic Orchestra in 2016. (PHOTO BY KEN KAISER / COURTESY OF THE MICHIGAN PHILHARMONIC)

The author with the Choate Rosemary Hall Orchestra at the St. Andrä Church in Salzburg, Austria. (PHOTO BY ELIZABETH MAIHOCK BELOFF)

The author with The Wallingford Symphony Orchestra performing *The Dove Tale* in 2017. (PHOTO BY ELIZABETH MAIHOCK BELOFF)

Top: *Jim Beloff: Two Ukulele Concertos* CD cover. (COURTESY OF FLEA MARKET MUSIC, INC.)

Bottom: *Liz and Jim Beloff: Rare Air* CD cover (COURTESY OF FLEA MARKET MUSIC, INC.)

TWO UKULELE CONCERTOS
Works For Solo Ukulele & Symphony Orchestra

UKE CAN'T BE SERIOUS

The Dove Tale

Also featuring the song
CHARLES IVES

By JIM BELOFF
Orchestrations by JASON NYBERG & RICK CUNHA

rare air

liz & jim beloff

The *Two Ukulele Concertos* EP was the tenth of eleven CDs we'd released on our Flea Market Music label. Others include *Rare Air*, a CD Liz and I recorded in 2009 with many of the Boston musicians who played on the *Paradise Lost & Found* sessions. Coproduced by WAITIKI bassist, Randy Wong, most of the songs on the CD were originals, including "Old in New Mexico," a song I'd written with Lyle Ritz. The rest were covers that we often performed live, like "The Glory of Love" and "Tonight You Belong to Me." "Que Sera, Sera" was another cover that Liz sang slower than the Doris Day version. By slowing the tempo, the song became deeper and more touching. Because Liz has a honeyed voice similar to Doris Day, live performances of the song always seemed to transport audiences, especially those who remembered the original recording.

Dreams I Left in Pockets was a two-CD set I put out in 2014. Recorded by Rick Cunha, it featured thirty-three of my songs written alone or cowritten with Herb Ohta, Lyle Ritz, and Kim Oler. Encoded on each disc were PDFs of the actual music—melody, lyrics, and chords—that could be printed out from a computer. That was in

Jim Beloff: Dreams I Left in Pockets CD cover (COURTESY OF FLEA MARKET MUSIC, INC.)

203

Lyle Ritz: No Frills CD cover (COURTESY OF FLEA MARKET MUSIC, INC.)

response to periodic requests for the sheet music to my songs. Lyle Ritz also recorded *No Frills*, a solo CD, for Flea Market Music. It was recorded in his home on an Apple iBook G4 in 2006. This was the first album where Lyle was able to play both the ukulele and bass parts and he was especially pleased with the results.

Just before the pandemic hit in January 2020, I recorded ten songs for a new solo album at The Coffeehouse, a studio in Middletown, Connecticut. The original plan was to bring in local musicians to flesh out the basic tracks. Once the lockdown kicked in, I figured that would have to wait. Then I began to think about some of the extraordinary Los Angeles–based musicians I'd recorded with in the past and wondered if I might be able to work with them remotely. I sent the rough tracks to Randy Landas, who had played bass on the *Dreams* CDs, and he was able to record his parts from home. He then forwarded those tracks to several of his local musician friends, who added their parts remotely. Two months later, the finished tracks were sent back for final mixing and mastering and *The Wind and Sun* was released in August 2020.

The title song of *The Wind and Sun* was inspired by my favorite Aesop's fable, which seems more relevant than ever. Of the remaining nine songs, two were collaborations with Herb Ohta and two were songs I'd written for Bill Macy projects including, "I Don't Want to Drink Alone."

The distinctive cover art for *The Wind and Sun* was by Scott Baldwin, with whom I'd worked in 2017 on a long-gestating project, a book of my palindromes. A palindrome is a word or phrase that reads the same way forward or backward. Much in the way I've enjoyed the lyric writing challenges imposed by perfect rhymes and scansion, I've also been drawn to the constraints of certain kinds of wordplay, like palindromes. The best ones have a certain coherence, such as Leigh Mercer's classic "A man, a plan a canal: Panama!" For more than thirty years I wrote these odd symmetrical lines with the idea that someday, if I had enough good ones, I'd put them in a book. Although there have been many illustrated collections published over the years, I wanted the artwork that accompanied the palindromes to be symmetrical. When I proposed this to Scott Baldwin, he rose to the challenge. To facilitate this, he carved half images on

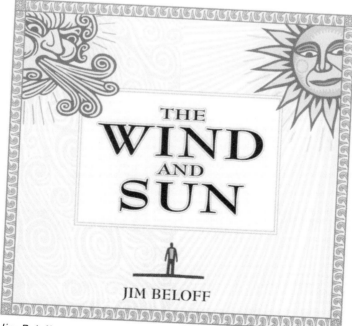

Jim Beloff: The Wind and Sun CD cover. (COURTESY OF FLEA MARKET MUSIC, INC.)

linoleum blocks and then imported them into his computer where they were flopped and colored, creating perfectly symmetrical art. The resulting self-published, limited edition book, *One's Reverses, Reverse. No?* featured forty-four of my best palindromes. Here are a few examples:

- Lapses? Order red roses, pal.
- No-no is I've let a television on.
- Oh, who is as selfless as I? Oh who?
- Eli began a motel bible to manage bile.
- Gal, if on a familiar trail I'm a fan of, I lag."

Will Shortz, the *New York Times* Crossword Puzzle Editor, is a fan of all wordplay and he sent along this quote: "Some of the best illustrated palindromes I've seen. The palindromes make sense, and the pictures are funny!" I haven't come up with any good "ukulele" palindromes yet, but, interestingly, the first and last three letters of the word are symmetrical.

ONE'S REVERSES, REVERSE. NO?

44 Palindromes by Jim Beloff

One's Reverses, Reverse. No? cover. (COURTESY OF FLEA MARKET MUSIC, INC.)

Revel Lad! Light a Path. Gild All, Ever.

It may be early to be thinking about an epitaph, but at the moment I'm leaning toward a palindrome of mine: "Revel lad! Light a path. Gild all, ever." So far, this ukulele adventure has largely been one of revelry and, in many ways, I feel we did light a path and spread that glow to others. In recent years, I've been acknowledged for these contributions: The Australian and British ukulele magazines *Kamuke* and *UKE* have both inducted me into their Hall of Fame, and *Ukulele* magazine put me on the cover of their fall 2018 issue. Under the headline, "Love at First Strum," writer Audrey Coleman added the subheadline, "From the flea market to meeting a Beatle, the ukulele changed Jim Beloff's life, and then he changed ours."

Ukulele magazine cover, Fall 2018.
(PHOTO BY MARILYN CATSUS / COURTESY OF STRINGLETTER MEDIA)

Hillel Wasserman, a friend of ours from Los Angeles, once said that rather than "aging gracefully," he was "aging gratefully." That was so good, I turned it into a song. Over the years, I've learned that songs are efficient delivery systems for wise thoughts and sage advice and that ukuleles are a great delivery system for songs. What I've also noticed—now that I have committed this journey to words and images—are the many remarkable moments of good luck and timing. So many unexpected connections, fortuitous meetings, foreshadowings, and coincidences make me wonder whether it was all prearranged, somehow.

Amazingly, the third wave continues to roll on. No cycle lasts forever and yet we're now more than twenty years into this wave and it shows no sign of slowing. The ukulele market is still a bright spot in the music store universe, and it seems like a new young uke star is acclaimed every six months. In the November 2020 issue of *MMR*, the music trade magazine, they wrote how guitar sales are soaring due to the pandemic. At the same time, they wondered how long that might last. I couldn't help but smile at this sentence: "Most trends (with the exception of the ukulele craze, apparently) peter out, of course—what comes up must come down and all that."

And we are ever so grateful. I never expected the Rose Bowl Martin tenor uke to lead us where it did, but we're very happy to be here. To everyone who has supported our efforts along the way, who bought our books and our music, attended workshops and concerts, we offer our profound thanks. To earn a living through music is a privilege and we try to never forget that. We are indebted to all the many wonderful, talented partners, friends, and family who helped and inspired us along the way.

"Walk Each Other Home," the last song on *The Wind and Sun* album, was written early in 2020 and inspired by a line from Ram Dass, "We're all just walking each other home." Wherever this adventure leads next, we know we'll be in good company.

208

Liz and Jim performing at the Martha's Vineyard Ukulele Festival in October 2015.
(COURTESY OF FEATHERSTONE CENTER FOR THE ARTS AND MARTHA'S VINEYARD UKULELE FESTIVAL)

(AUTHOR'S COLLECTION)

From the moment of our birth,
We count down our time on earth.
Peaks and valleys we shall roam,
As we walk each other home.

Try to take it all in stride,
Step by step and side by side,
Steady as a metronome,
As we walk each other home.

Days of sunshine,
Days of showers,
We shall share them all.

From the moment of our birth,
We count down our time on earth.
Peaks and valleys we shall roam,
As we walk each other home.

NOW PUBLISHED WEEKLY

AUG. 23, 1927

Sweetheart Stories

15¢

HIS
UKULELE
LADY

(AUTHOR'S COLLECTION)

Thank You

First and foremost, to John Cerullo, Rowman & Littlefield, and Globe Pequot for saying "yes" to this book. The idea had been percolating for a while, but I'm not sure it would have gone any further without a contract and a deadline. To Ronny Schiff who has been there from the very beginning: editing, agenting, teaching, and friending. Thanks also to the following for helping me fact-check and confirm some of the events: Trish Dulka, Jeff Schroedl, Sarah Weeks, Eliane Reese, Pat Enos, Peter Thomas, Susan McCormick, Tony Cappa, John Chandler, Kora "Koko" Peterson, Peter Wingerd, Phyllis and Dale Webb, Larry Morton, and Elaine Godowsky. To Greg Olwell, Blair Jackson, Cameron Murray, Matt Warnes, Jason Verlinde, Nina Trevens, Ashley Knowles, Frank Döring, Lori O'Brien, Chris Rowan, and Harrison Levenstein for permission to include your photographs, digital images, and media. For additional permission assistance thanks to: Marianna McKee, Gene Sculatti, Gene Lee, David Ponak, Christian Wismuller, James Grupenhoff, Marilyn Catasus, Karen Loria, and James Wojcik. A big thanks also to Carol Flannery, Barbara Claire, and Jessica Thwaite from Rowman & Littlefield.

To Mom and Dad for all the encouragement and feedback.
And, to Liz for sharing this journey and your photographs.

Lyric Credits

"Big in Japan"
Lyrics and Music by Jim Beloff
Copyright © 1995 Flea Market Music, Inc.

"Can't Help But Smile"
Lyrics and Music by Jim Beloff
Copyright © 2004 Flea Market Music, Inc.

"Charles Ives"
Lyrics and Music by Jim Beloff
Copyright © 1994 Flea Market Music, Inc.

"Flea Market Monkey"
Lyrics and Music by Jim Beloff
Copyright © 1993 Flea Market Music, Inc.

"Uke Can't Be Serious"
Lyrics and Music by Jim Beloff
Copyright © 1999 Flea Market Music, Inc.

"UKEtopia"
Lyrics and Music by Jim Beloff
Copyright © 1999 Flea Market Music, Inc.

"Ukulele and You, A"
Lyrics and Music by Jim Beloff
Copyright © 2005 Flea Market Music, Inc.

(AUTHOR'S COLLECTION)

Music Books by Jim Beloff

Jumpin' Jim's Ukulele Favorites, Flea Market Music, Inc. (1992)
ISBN 978-0-7935-2050-3

Jumpin' Jim's Ukulele Tips 'N' Tunes: A Beginner's Method and Songbook, Flea Market
Music, Inc. (1994) ISBN 978-0-7935-3377-0

Jumpin' Jim's Ukulele Gems, Flea Market Music, Inc. (1995) ISBN 978-0-7935-5796-7

Jumpin' Jim's Ukulele Christmas, Flea Market Music, Inc. (1998)
ISBN 978-0-7935-9486-3

Jumpin' Jim's Gone Hawaiian, Flea Market Music, Inc. (1999)
ISBN 978-0-634-00934-1

Jumpin' Jim's '60s Uke-In, Flea Market Music, Inc. (1999) ISBN 978-0-634-00631-9

Jumpin' Jim's Camp Ukulele, Flea Market Music, Inc. (2000) ISBN 978-0-634-01850-3

Jumpin' Jim's Ukulele Beach Party, Flea Market Music, Inc. (2001)
ISBN 978-0-634-03425-1

Jumpin' Jim's Ukulele Masters: Lyle Ritz, Flea Market Music, Inc. (2001)
ISBN 978-0-634-02764-2

*Jumpin' Jim's Ukulele Masters: Lyle Ritz Solos: 15 Chord Solos Arranged by the Ukulele Jazz
Master*, Flea Market Music, Inc. (2002) ISBN 978-0-634-04658-2

Jumpin' Jim's Ukulele Masters: Herb Ohta, Flea Market Music, Inc. (2002)
ISBN 978-0-634-03863-1

Jumpin' Jim's Ukulele Spirit, Flea Market Music, Inc. (2002) ISBN 978-0-634-04618-6

Jumpin' Jim's Gone Hollywood, Flea Market Music, Inc. (2003)
ISBN 978-0-634-06218-6

Jumpin' Jim's Ukulele Masters: John King — The Classical Ukulele, Flea Market Music,
Inc. (2004) ISBN 978-0-634-07979-5

Jumpin' Jim's Ukulele Island, Flea Market Music, Inc. (2004) ISBN 978-0-634-07980-1

Jumpin' Jim's the Bari Best, Flea Market Music, Inc. (2005) ISBN 978-1-4234-0706-5

Jumpin' Jim's Ukulele Country, Flea Market Music, Inc. (2005)
ISBN 978-1-4234-0122-3

Jumpin' Jim's Happy Holidays, Flea Market Music, Inc. (2006)
ISBN 978-1-4234-2249-5

Ukulele Fretboard Roadmaps, Fred Sokolow/Jim Beloff, Hal Leonard LLC (2006)
ISBN 978-1-4234-0041-7

Jumpin' Jim's Ukulele Masters: Lyle Lite: 16 Easy Chord Solos Arranged by Ukulele Jazz Master Lyle Ritz, Flea Market Music, Inc. (2008) ISBN 978-1-4234-3781-9

Blues Ukulele, arr. by Fred Sokolow, Flea Market Music, Inc. (2008)
ISBN 978-1-4234-6572-0

Elvis Presley for Ukulele, (arranger) Hal Leonard LLC (2009) ISBN 978-1-4234-6556-0

Disney Songs for Ukulele, (arranger) Hal Leonard LLC (2010)
ISBN 978-1-4234-9560-4

Bluegrass Ukulele, arr. by Fred Sokolow, Flea Market Music, Inc. (2010)
ISBN 978-1-4234-9316-7

The Daily Ukulele, Hal Leonard LLC and Flea Market Music, Inc. (2010)
ISBN 978-1-4234-7775-4

Rodgers & Hammerstein for Ukulele, (arranger) Hal Leonard LLC (2011)
ISBN 978-1-61780-386-4

From Lute to Uke, arr. by Tony Mizen, Flea Market Music, Inc. (2011)
ISBN 978-1-4584-0651-4

Broadway Classics for Ukulele, (arranger) Hal Leonard LLC (2012)
ISBN 978-1-4584-1565-3

The Baroque Ukulele, arr. by Tony Mizen, Flea Market Music, Inc. (2012)
ISBN 978-1-4768-1520-6

The Daily Ukulele: Leap Year Edition, Hal Leonard LLC and Flea Market Music, Inc. (2012) ISBN 978-1-4584-8268-6

The Daily Ukulele: Baritone Edition, Hal Leonard LLC and Flea Market Music, Inc. (2013) ISBN 978-1-4803-5200-1

Jazzing Up the Ukulele, Fred Sokolow, Flea Market Music, Inc. (2015)
ISBN 978-1-4803-9528-2

The Romantic Ukulele, arr. by Tony Mizen, Flea Market Music, Inc. (2015)
ISBN 978-1-4950-2254-8

The Daily Ukulele To Go!, Hal Leonard LLC and Flea Market Music, Inc. (2015)
ISBN 978-1-4803-4227-9

The Daily Ukulele: Leap Year Edition for Baritone Ukulele, Hal Leonard LLC and Flea
Market Music, Inc. (2017) ISBN 978-1-4950-8595-6

Jumpin' Jim's Ukulele Masters: James Hill—Duets for One, Flea Market Music, Inc.
(2017) ISBN 978-1540003041

Books by Jim Beloff

Beloff, Jim: *The Ukulele—A Visual History*, Miller Freeman (1997) ISBN
978-0-87930-454-6

Beloff, Jim: *The Ukulele—A Visual History*, Backbeat Books, 2nd Edition (2003)
ISBN 978-0-87930-758-5

Beloff, Jim: *One's Reverses, Reverse. No? 44 Palindromes* (Limited Printing), Jim Beloff
(2017)

Discography by Jim Beloff

Beloff, Jim: Jim's Dog Has Fleas, Flea Market Music, 1993 (AVL93117CD)

Legends of Ukulele, (producer), Rhino Records, 1998 (R2 75278)

Beloff, Jim: For the Love of Uke, Flea Market Music, 1998 (FMM 1002)

Beloff, Jim: It's a Fluke—A Five Song Sampler on Four Strings, Flea Market Music, 1999 (FMM 1003)

Ritz, Lyle, Ohta, Herb: A Night of Ukulele Jazz—Live at McCabe's (producer) Flea Market Music, 2001 (FMM 1004)

Various Artists, *The Finer Things, The Songs of Herb Ohta and Jim Beloff*, Flea Market Music, 2004 (FMM 1005)

Ritz, Lyle: No Frills, (producer) Flea Market Music, 2006 (FMM 1006)

Various Artists, *Paradise Lost & Found*, Flea Market Music, 2007 (FMM 1007)

Beloff, Jim and Liz: Rare Air, Flea Market Music, 2009 (FMM 1008)

Beloff, Jim: Dreams I Left in Pockets: 33 Songs by Jim Beloff, 2-CD set, Flea Market Music, 2014 (FMM 1009)

Beloff, Jim: Two Ukulele Concertos, Flea Market Music, 2018 (FMM 1010)

Beloff, Jim: The Wind and Sun, Flea Market Music, 2020 (FMM 1011)

DVDs by Jim Beloff

Beloff, Jim: The Joy of Uke—Volume 1, Homespun Tapes (1998) ISBN 978-1-932537-24-6

Beloff, Jim: The Joy of Uke—Volume 2, Moving Beyond the Basics, Homespun Tapes (2003) ISBN 978-1-932537-25-2

Lyle's Style: Ukulele Master Lyle Ritz Shares a Lifetime of Performance Techniques, (producer) Flea Market Music (2009) ISBN 978-1-4234-7457-9

Jumpin' Jim's Ukulele Workshop, Homespun (2011) ISBN 978-1-59773-318-2

Recommended Listening: To hear many of the songs referenced in the book, go to the *UKEtopia* playlist on Spotify.

Index of Songs

Index

(PHOTO BY ATTILA ASZODI)